Flavors of
Southeast Asia
Recipes from Indonesia, Thailand & Vietnam

Indonesia
Maudie Horsting & Frona de Lannoy

Thailand
Jeffrey Davis

Vietnam
Lan Cao

101 Productions
San Francisco

Note about metric: Measurements in this book are not straight conversions from U.S. measurements to metric, but have been adapted into metric for each individual recipe.

Note about spelling: The names of the recipes have been given in the dominant language of the country, followed by an English name or description. Spelling of the foreign language names in this book and other sources will vary because of phonetic interpretation (as in the case of Thailand) and recent standardization within the country (as in the case of Indonesian and Malaysian introduction of unified spelling). The local name for an ingredient is sometimes given in addition to the English name. For example, fish sauce is *nam bla* in Thailand, *nuoc mam* in Vietnam. This is to familiarize the reader with the foreign names of the principal ingredients of each country. For a complete list of ingredients, see the glossary beginning on page 156.

Printed and bound in the United States of America. Distributed to the Book trade in the United States by Charles Scribner's Sons, New York.

Published by 101 Productions
834 Mission Street
San Francisco, California 94103

Library of Congress Cataloging in Publication Data
Main entry under title:

Flavors of Southeast Asia.

Includes index.
1. Cookery, Indonesian.   2. Cookery, Thai.
3. Cookery, Vietnamese.   I. Horsting, Maudie, 1930-
TX 724.515F56   641.5'959   79-22341
ISBN 0-89286-159-2

Contents

Though the following recipes are from Indonesia, Thailand and Vietnam, the three most popular Southeast Asian cuisines in the United States, the drawings are from the artist's travels throughout Southeast Asia, principally Singapore and Malaysia.

INDONESIA

The Indonesian Meal

At various times in history, Indonesia, with its over 13,000 islands, has been colonized or influenced by the Dutch, English, Portuguese, Indians and Chinese. Its own natural diversity combined with the presence of these cultures has created a rich and varied cuisine.

A Westerner's usual introduction to Indonesian cuisine is the *rijsttafel*, or "rice table." It is, in simple terms, rice accompanying a wide variety of dishes, and is one tradition borne of the Dutch colonization of Indonesia that remains popular in Holland. The *rijsttafel* is so popular in Holland, the Dutch have even coined a verb for it—*rijsttafelen*, to go "ricetabling."

An Indonesian meal need not be as elaborate as a *rijsttafel*, however, to be enjoyed. For a simple meal, serve one dry *sambal goreng* (fried *sambal*), one *sambal goreng* with liquid, a vegetable dish *(sajor)*, a meat, poultry or seafood dish and whatever condiments you desire. Add some fresh cucumber slices and you have a simple meal fit for royalty. For an elaborate dinner, increase the variety of dishes, perhaps three kinds of meat or seafood dishes and assorted side dishes, and you have a meal for a celebration, a *slametan* (see page 8).

The word *sambal* occurs in any discussion of Indonesian cuisine and the term is a complex one. Some believe it comes from the word "jumble" and was adapted from the language of the colonizers. In the most general sense it implies a chopped mixture of ingredients that are fried together. It can be a condiment or a seasoning in dishes, such as *sambal badjak*, or a side dish, such as *sambal goreng tomaat*.

For a simple meal, set the table with a plate, fork and spoon. Indonesians traditionally eat with the fingers of the right hand—making little balls of the rice and scooping up the foods with them, then facilely transporting it all to the mouth. Most Indonesians are, however, familiar with the Western use of utensils and many eat that way today. A more elaborate meal calls for a knife resting on a knife horse, a holder much like a miniature sawhorse of silver or crystal, fingerbowls and table linens.

Dinners are not begun with soup, like a Western meal, but rather all of the dishes are brought to the table at once. If a soup is served, it is generally a special soup, such as *soto ajam*, served over rice with condiments, and it is a complete meal.

Meals are ended with fresh fruit. The islands offer an almost infinite variety. There are plump, rosy mangoes, at least six different varieties, each with a distinctive flavor. The rambutan, a small fruit that grows in clusters, has a reddish skin covered with short spines and firm, transparent flesh with a pleasant sweet taste. Salak, shaped like a spinning top, is dark, shiny brown on the outside and yellow and tart on the inside. The crown-topped mangosteen has purplish, leathery skin covering creamy white, segmented flesh. The flesh is sweet, fragrant and melts on the tongue. And the king of fruit, the durian. It is a massive, often times 20 inches (50 cm) in diameter and 30 inches (75 cm) in length, with gray-green skin covered with spines. It announces its ripeness by giving off an overpowering yeasty fragrance that is offensive to many Westerners but cherished by most Southeast Asians. Inside this giant fruit are many segments of creamy, soft flesh surrounding a pit. As the story goes, people can get drunk from eating it.

The importance of fruit as dessert does not preclude the Indonesians' fondness for sweets. Cookies, candies and pastries are enjoyed for afternoon breaks, or whenever the fancy strikes.

ABOUT THE RECIPES

The recipes that follow are designed to serve four to six persons, unless otherwise specified. They can, of course, be easily increased or decreased in size according to the size of your party. All of them are of Javanese origin, perhaps the most complex of the Indonesian cuisines. Dishes from the other islands are very similar to those of Java, the differences principally being in the combinations of spices. It is the complexity of Javanese food and our familiarity with the cuisine that is the reason for this concentration.

Many of the seasonings used—ground ginger, nutmeg and coriander—are readily available in any supermarket. The more exotic ones, such as *laos* and *sereh,* are more difficult to locate, but can be obtained at specialty markets. Both Conimex and Runel brand are very good choices when purchasing these ingredients. Though coconut oil is commonly used in Indonesia, vegetable oil has been substituted here because it is easier to find, less expensive and an excellent substitute. Peanut oil would also be suitable.

Rice

NASI KOENING
Yellow Rice

Sometimes for the birth of a child, the start of a new venture or some other important occasion, people give a special dinner called a *slametan*. The purpose of the dinner is to ward off the evil spirits and to secure the support of the good ones. *Nasi koening* is often a part of a *slametan* and is elaborately presented on round split-bamboo trays with an abundance of garnishes.

2 cups (500 ml) long-grain white rice
1-1/3 cups (325 ml) coconut milk
2/3 cup (150 ml) water
1/2 teaspoon (3 ml) ground turmeric
Lemon grass stalk *(sereh),* fresh or dried
1 bay leaf
1 dried citrus leaf *(djeroek poeroet)*
1/2 teaspoon (3 ml) salt

Garnishes
1 cucumber, thinly sliced
3 eggs, hard-cooked and sliced
2 tablespoons (30 ml) French-fried onions

Wash the rice in cold water until the water runs clear; drain well. Put the rice into a 2-quart (2 L) saucepan with a tightly fitting lid. Mix together the coconut milk, water, turmeric, lemon grass, bay leaf, citrus leaf and salt and add to the saucepan. Bring to a boil and stir briefly. Reduce heat, cover and cook over low heat until all of the water is absorbed. If at this point the rice is not quite tender, add about 1/4 cup (60 ml) boiling water, cover and cook over low heat until water is evaporated. The entire cooking process should take about 30 minutes. Fluff the rice with a fork and transfer to a large platter. Garnish with the cucumber and egg slices and sprinkle with the French-fried onions.

Nasi Goering (Savory Rice) Proceed as directed above, omitting the turmeric, lemon grass, bay leaf, citrus leaf and garnishes.

Note For a grand *nasi koening* or *nasi goering* dinner, the following recipes are the best choices to make it a success: Boemboe Bali (page 34), Soto Ajam I (page 29), Ajam Ketjap (page 30), Ajam Boemboe Opor (page 31), Ajam Boemboe Roedjak (page 32), Kerrie Ikan (page 28), Brengkesan (page 26), Oblok-Oblok (page 17), Sambal Goreng Tomaat (page 19) and Sajor Lodeh (page 24).

NASI DJAGOENG
Rice and Corn

In some parts of Indonesia, among them the island of Madura, corn is mixed into the rice. This practice is not only a question of taste, but also of economy. Corn has always been plentiful and is cheaper than rice.

The easiest way to prepare rice and corn is to cook the white rice as you would if you were making it plain, and when the water is almost evaporated, stir in 1/2 cup (125 ml) fresh or frozen corn kernels for every 2 cups (500 ml) raw rice. Be sure to add a little salt to the cooking water.

NASI GORENG
Fried Rice

This dish must have been born out of the need for a concoction in which one could combine all the leftovers.

3 tablespoons (45 ml) vegetable oil
3 tablespoons (45 ml) grated onion
4 garlic cloves, minced
1 heaping teaspoon (6 ml) *sambal badjak*
1/2 teaspoon (3 ml) salt
1 cup (250 ml) diced cooked meat (beef, pork, ham, chicken or any combination)
2 tablespoons (30 ml) Indonesian-style soy sauce *(ketjap)*
3 cups (750 ml) cooked long-grain white rice

Garnishes
2 tablespoons (30 ml) French-fried onions
Omelet strips (following)
Cucumber slices

Heat the oil in a wok or skillet, add the onion, garlic, *sambal badjak* and salt and stir-fry until onion is translucent. Add the meat and soy sauce and stir-fry about 15 minutes. Then add the rice, mix well and heat through. Taste and adjust seasoning with salt. Transfer to a platter and sprinkle with French-fried onions. Arrange the omelet strips over the rice in a lattice pattern and ring with cucumber slices.

Omelet Beat together 2 eggs and 1-1/2 teaspoons (7 ml) water. Heat a little butter in a large skillet and pour in the egg mixture, lifting and tilting the pan so that the entire bottom surface is covered. The omelet should be very thin and crêpelike. When the egg is set, slide the omelet from the pan. Let cool, roll up into a cylinder and cut crosswise into thin strips.

Variation If you want to try a fancy version of this dish, add crab meat or shrimp meat and ham in place of the leftover meat. It will be worthy of a banquet. Also, if the dish seems a bit dry when it is cooked, mix in a little butter.

Sambals & Vegetables

SAMBAL BADJAK
Chili Pepper and Onion Sambal

This *sambal* is an important ingredient in many of the recipes in this book. Though traditionally fresh chili peppers and onions are used, dried ones are used here for convenience, since fresh red chili peppers are difficult to find year round. If you wish to use fresh ingredients, proceed as directed but alter measures to 2 cups (500 ml) pulverized chili peppers and 2-1/2 cups (625 ml) pulverized onions.

1-1/2 cups (375 ml) crushed dried red chili
    peppers*
2 cups (500 ml) dried onion flakes
1-1/2 cups (375 ml) vegetable oil
1 bay leaf
A few snips dried citrus leaf *(djeroek poeroet)*

Spice mixture
1 teaspoon (5 ml) galangal powder *(laos)*
1/4 teaspoon (1 ml) ground lemon grass *(sereh)*
1 teaspoon (5 ml) sugar
1 heaping teaspoon (6 ml) salt
5 kemiri nuts
Dried shrimp paste *(trassi)* the size of a peanut
Tamarind pulp *(asem)*, seeded, the size of a peanut

Combine the chili and onions in a bowl and add water to just cover; let stand a few minutes. Combine all the ingredients for the spice mixture in a mortar or blender container and blend until smooth; set aside. Heat the oil in a deep saucepan or wok until very hot, then remove from the heat. Drain excess water off the chilies and onions and add to the oil with the bay leaf, citrus leaf and spice mixture. Return the pan to the heat and bring to a boil. Reduce heat and simmer, stirring frequently, for about 2 hours. At this point the mixture should be deep red in color. Cool thoroughly and store in airtight jars. The *sambal* will keep for months in the refrigerator.

*Crushed chili pepper is available in bottles in most supermarkets.

Note If you don't want to go to this much trouble, Runel brand *sambal badjak* is an excellent substitute.

BAWANG GORENG
French-fried Onions

These onions are an important garnish and flavoring for many Indonesian dishes. The simplest way to prepare them is with minced *dried* onions. Fill a fine mesh strainer about half full with the onions and immerse the strainer in hot vegetable oil until they turn golden brown. This will take only a few seconds. Lift the strainer out immediately and drain the onions on paper toweling. Let cool, then store in airtight containers.

If you wish to start with fresh onions, slice them *very* thin. Each slice must be of uniform thickness or the onions will not cook evenly and you will end up with some burned ones and others that are undercooked. Fry the onion slices in deep hot oil until golden brown. This will take some time as all of the moisture must cook out. When ready, lift out, drain on paper toweling, cool and store in airtight containers.

REMPEJEH
Rice Flour Cookie with Peanuts

These cookies should be very thin and crisp. They are good as a snack, as an accompaniment to beverages or with curries and rice.

1/2 cup (125 ml) roasted peanuts
Vegetable oil for deep-frying

Batter
1 cup (250 ml) regular rice flour
1 teaspoon (5 ml) garlic powder
1 teaspoon (5 ml) ground coriander
1/2 teaspoon (3 ml) ground cumin
1/2 teaspoon (3 ml) ground turmeric
1/2 teaspoon (3 ml) galangal powder *(laos)*
1/2 teaspoon (3 ml) salt
1 to 1-1/2 cups (250 to 375 ml) coconut milk

Mix together all of the ingredients for the batter, starting with 1 cup (250 ml) coconut milk. If the batter is too thick add more coconut milk until it is a rather thin consistency. Heat oil to a depth of 1/2 inch (1.5 cm) in a wok or skillet and drop in 1 teaspoon (5 ml) batter. Fry until golden, then taste and adjust seasoning with salt. Now mix the peanuts into the batter and drop the batter by tablespoonfuls (15 ml) into the hot oil, 2 or 3 at a time. Fry until golden, then remove with a slotted utensil and drain on paper toweling.

SERCENDENG
Roasted Coconut with Peanuts

Excellent accompaniment for curries and yellow rice.

3 tablespoons (45 ml) vegetable oil
3-1/2 cups (875 ml) grated fresh coconut meat, or
   3 cups (750 ml) unsweetened dried grated
   coconut, mixed with 1 cup (250 ml) water
     and soaked a few minutes
1/2 cup (125 ml) Spanish peanuts

Spice mixture
1 heaping teaspoon (6 ml) salt
1 teaspoon (5 ml) sugar
1 teaspoon (5 ml) distilled white vinegar
2 teaspoons (10 ml) ground coriander
1 teaspoon (5 ml) ground cumin
1 medium onion, chopped
5 garlic cloves, or
   2 teaspoons (10 ml) garlic powder
Dried shrimp paste *(trassi)* the size of a peanut
5 kemiri nuts

Combine all the ingredients for the spice mixture in a mortar or a blender container and blend until smooth. (If using a blender and the motor begins to labor, add a little water.) Heat the oil in a wok or skillet, add the spice mixture and stir-fry a few minutes. Transfer the pan to a preheated 275° to 300°F (140° to 150°C) oven and bake 2 hours or until golden brown, stirring frequently. Remove from the oven and stir in the peanuts. Store in an airtight container. This will keep several months.

FRIKADEL DJAGOENG
Corn Fritters

1-1/2 cups (375 ml) fresh or thawed frozen corn
   kernels
3 green onions, chopped
Vegetable oil for frying

Batter
1 cup (250 ml) regular rice flour
1 egg, beaten
3/4 cup (175 ml) water

Spice mixture
1/2 teaspoon (3 ml) ground coriander
1/4 teaspoon (1 to 2 ml) ground cumin
1 teaspoon (5 ml) salt
1/2 teaspoon (3 ml) ground black pepper

Mix together all of the ingredients for the batter. Combine all of the spices and mix into the batter. When the batter is smooth, mix in the corn kernels and onions. Add oil to a skillet to a depth of about 1/4 inch (6 mm) and heat until hot. Drop the batter into the oil by heaping tablespoonfuls (20 ml), cooking 2 or 3 at a time, and fry until nicely browned and crisp on the edges. Lift the fritters out with a slotted utensil and drain on paper toweling.

Note If you want to make very crisp fritters, omit the egg from the batter and increase the water to 1 cup (250 ml).

TAHOE KETJAP
Soybean Cake in Soy Sauce

Soybean cake is an excellent substitute for meat. For a light dinner, serve this as a one-dish meal.

2 quarts (2 L) water
1 teaspoon (5 ml) salt
2 tablespoons (30 ml) distilled white vinegar
1-1/2 pounds (750 g) fresh bean curd cakes
Vegetable oil for deep-frying
2 cups (500 ml) bean sprouts, blanched 1 minute
   and well drained
3 eggs, hard cooked and sliced
1 tablespoon (15 ml) French-fried onions

Sauce
1/4 cup (60 ml) Indonesian-style soy sauce
   (ketjap)
1 cup (250 ml) water
1 tablespoon (15 ml) shrimp sauce *(petis)*
1 teaspoon (5 ml) sugar
1 teaspoon (5 ml) *sambal badjak*
1/2 teaspoon (3 ml) salt
1 teaspoon (5 ml) fresh lemon juice
1/2 teaspoon (3 ml) garlic powder

Combine all the ingredients for the sauce in a saucepan and mix well. Cook over medium heat, stirring often, until the mixture is reduced by half; set aside. Put the water, salt and vinegar in a saucepan, add the bean curd cakes, bring to a boil, reduce heat and cook gently about 10 minutes. Carefully remove the bean curd cakes from the saucepan and drain well, gently pressing out as much of the water as possible. Cut the bean curd cakes into 1-inch (3 cm) cubes. Heat oil to a depth of about 1 inch (3 cm) in a wok or skillet until very hot (375°F or 190°C). Deep-fry the bean cake until lightly golden. Remove with a slotted utensil and drain on paper toweling. Arrange the bean sprouts on a serving platter and put the bean curd cubes on top. Pour the sauce over all and garnish with the egg slices and French-fried onions.

SAMBAL TEMPEH
Spicy Soybean Cake

This is real peasant fare and provides a very interesting contrast in texture and taste.

1 *tempeh* cake, about 5 inches (13 cm) square and
   1 inch (3 cm) thick
3 or 4 fresh red chili peppers, seeded
1/2 teaspoon (3 ml) salt
Dried shrimp paste *(trassi)* the size of a peanut
Juice of 1 small lemon

Slice the *tempeh* in half so that you have two 5-inch (13 cm) squares 1/2 inch (1.5 cm) wide. Place the *tempeh* under a broiler and broil on both sides until rather dark. Remove from the broiler and crumble in a bowl; set aside. Combine the peppers, salt, trassi and lemon juice in a mortar or blender container and blend until smooth. Thoroughly mix the pepper mixture with the crumbled *tempeh*.

OBLOK-OBLOK
Soybean Cake with Coconut Milk

1 tablespoon (15 ml) vegetable oil
12 ounces (400 g) fresh bean curd cakes, cut into
    1-inch (3 cm) cubes
1 bay leaf
1 fresh long green chili pepper, seeded and cut into
    julienne, or
    1/2 green bell pepper, seeded and cut into
    julienne
1 cup (250 ml) water
1 cup (250 ml) coconut milk

Spice mixture
1/2 teaspoon (3 ml) ground aromatic ginger
    (kentjoer)
1/2 teaspoon (3 ml) galangal powder *(laos)*
1 teaspoon (5 ml) crunchy-style peanut butter
    without additives
1 heaping teaspoon (6 ml) *sambal badjak*
2 garlic cloves
1 tablespoon (15 ml) chopped onion
1 teaspoon (5 ml) salt
1 teaspoon (5 ml) sugar
1 teaspoon (5 ml) distilled white vinegar

Combine all the ingredients for the spice mixture in a mortar or a blender container and blend until smooth; set aside. Heat the oil in a good-sized saucepan and fry the spice mixture a few minutes. Add the bean curd cubes, bay leaf, pepper strips and water and cook over medium heat 10 minutes. Add the coconut milk and just heat through. Taste and adjust seasoning with salt before serving.

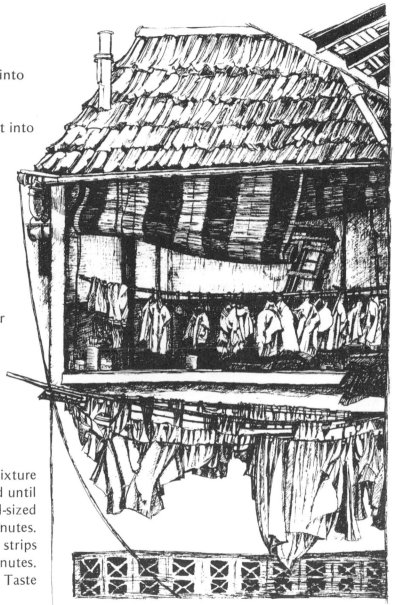

ASINAN
Sweet and Sour Cucumber Salad

3 large cucumbers, peeled and thinly sliced
1 medium onion, thinly sliced
1 fresh large red chili pepper, seeded and thinly
  sliced

Dressing
1/4 cup (60 ml) distilled white vinegar
1/4 cup (60 ml) vegetable oil
1/2 teaspoon (3 ml) salt
2 teaspoons (10 ml) sugar
1/2 teaspoon (3 ml) garlic powder

Put the cucumber slices in a shallow bowl, arrange
the onion slices on top and sprinkle with the chili
slices. Combine all the ingredients for the dressing,
mixing well. Taste and adjust seasoning with salt.
Pour the dressing over the onions and cucumbers
and refrigerate a few hours or overnight if possible
to allow flavors to blend.

TOMAAT KETJAP
Tomatoes in Soy Sauce

2 cups (500 ml) bean sprouts
4 large firm ripe tomatoes, sliced
1 tablespoon (15 ml) French-fried onions

Sauce
1/4 cup (60 ml) Indonesian-style soy sauce
  (ketjap)
1 teaspoon (5 ml) *sambal badjak*
Juice of 1 small lemon
Salt and sugar to taste

Make a bed of the bean sprouts on a large platter.
Arrange the tomato slices on top of the bean
sprouts. Mix together all the ingredients for the
sauce and pour over the tomato slices. Garnish
with French-fried onions.

GADO-GADO
Salad with Peanut Dressing

This sauce is served with all kinds of boiled or
steamed vegetables that are cooked until tender
but still firm. Select your favorites: green beans,
carrots, cabbage, broccoli, zucchini, Brussels
sprouts, cucumbers, bean sprouts, etc. For added
body, boil or steam potatoes in their jackets, then
peel and slice them and arrange them in a bowl
with the vegetables. If you want to make the salad
a whole meal, add some deep-fried bean curd
cubes. Garnish the salad with French-fried onions
and quartered hard-cooked eggs and serve the peanut dressing on the side. If you prefer a raw vegetable salad, try butter and iceberg lettuce, cucumber, bean sprouts and a grated carrot or two. Just
as delicious with the peanut dressing.

3 tablespoons (45 ml) crunchy-style peanut
  butter without additives
1 heaping teaspoon (6 ml) *sambal badjak*
1 teaspoon (5 ml) sugar
1/2 teaspoon (3 ml) salt
1 to 1-1/2 teaspoons (5 to 7 ml) distilled white
  vinegar
1 scant teaspoon (4 ml) garlic powder
1-1/2 cups (375 ml) water
1 cup (250 ml) coconut milk

Combine the peanut butter, *sambal badjak,* sugar, salt, vinegar, garlic powder and water in a saucepan and bring to a boil, stirring constantly. Reduce heat and simmer, continuing to stir, until liquid is reduced by half. Add the coconut milk and simmer about 15 minutes longer. Taste and adjust seasoning with salt. If the sauce is too thick, add a few spoonfuls of water.

Variation To make *petjel,* follow the above recipe, adding about 1/3 teaspoon (2 ml) ground aromatic ginger *(kentjoer)* to the dressing. Proceed as directed, using the salad ingredients, cooked or raw, described in the introductory note, but mix the dressing into the vegetables rather than serving it on the side.

SAMBAL GORENG LOMBOK IDJO
Green Peppers in Soybean Sauce

1 tablespoon (15 ml) vegetable oil
3 green bell peppers, seeded and cut into julienne
2 teaspoons (10 ml) distilled white vinegar
3 tablespoons (45 ml) soybean condiment (see asterisked note, page 43)

Spice mixture
1 medium onion, chopped
4 garlic cloves
1/2 teaspoon (3 ml) galangal powder *(laos)*
1/2 teaspoon (3 ml) sugar

Combine all the ingredients for the spice mixture in a mortar or blender container and blend until smooth. Heat the oil in a wok or skillet and stir-fry the spice mixture a few minutes. Add the peppers, vinegar and soybean condiment and cook over medium heat until the peppers are tender.

SAMBAL GORENG TOMAAT
Tomatoes in Coconut Milk

1 tablespoon (15 ml) vegetable oil
4 or 5 large unripe tomatoes (green or reddish green), sliced
6 ounces (200 g) small cooked shrimp
1 heaping teaspoon (6 ml) *sambal badjak*
1 cup (250 ml) coconut milk

Spice mixture
1 medium onion, chopped
4 garlic cloves
1/2 teaspoon (3 ml) galangal powder *(laos)*
Dried shrimp paste *(trassi)* the size of a peanut
1 teaspoon (5 ml) sugar
1/2 teaspoon (3 ml) salt

Combine all the ingredients for the spice mixture in a mortar or blender container and blend until smooth. Heat the oil in a wok or Dutch oven and stir-fry the spices a few minutes. Add the tomatoes, shrimp and *sambal badjak* and stir-fry 5 minutes. Add the coconut milk and heat through. Taste and adjust seasoning with salt.

DADAR TAHOE
Bean Cake Omelet

12 ounces (400 g) fresh bean curd cakes
3 slices bacon, diced
1 tablespoon (15 ml) chopped onion
2 garlic cloves, crushed, or
   2 teaspoons (10 ml) garlic powder
1 teaspoon (5 ml) ground ginger
4 eggs
1/2 teaspoon (3 ml) salt
1/2 teaspoon (3 ml) ground black pepper
1/2 teaspoon (3 ml) Indonesian-style soy sauce
   (ketjap)
2 green onions, thinly sliced

Press as much liquid from the bean curd cakes as possible by covering them with paper toweling and gently applying pressure. Mash the bean curd with a fork or shred in a food processor fitted with a medium shredding blade; set aside. Fry the bacon in a 10-inch (25 cm) skillet until crisp. Discard all but 1 tablespoon (15 ml) of the drippings and add the onion, garlic and ginger. Sauté a few minutes. Add the bean cake and cook over low heat 10 minutes. Beat the eggs with the salt, pepper and soy sauce and pour the mixture into the pan. Cover and cook over medium low heat until the egg is set. Uncover and loosen the edges of the omelet with a spatula to let the uncooked portion flow underneath every now and again. When a fork inserted in the center comes out clean, the omelet is ready. Slide onto a platter and garnish with green onions.

Variation Substitute 1/4 cup (60 ml) small cooked shrimp for the bacon. Use 1 tablespoon (15 ml) vegetable oil in place of the bacon drippings and sauté the shrimp with the onion and garlic. Proceed as directed in recipe.

ORAK ARIK
Cabbage Scramble

2 tablespoons (30 ml) vegetable oil
1 tablespoon (15 ml) chopped onion
3 garlic cloves, finely chopped
3 ounces (90 g) small cooked shrimp, diced
1/2 teaspoon (3 ml) salt
1/2 teaspoon (3 ml) ground black pepper
1/2 small head cabbage, very finely shredded
4 eggs, beaten
2 green onions, finely sliced

Heat the oil in a wok or skillet, add the onion, garlic, shrimp, salt and pepper and stir-fry until the onions are translucent. Mix in the cabbage and then add the eggs. Cook, stirring, until the eggs are set. Transfer to a serving dish and garnish with green onions.

PETJEL TERONG
Eggplant in Savory Sauce

2 large eggplants
1/4 cup (60 ml) distilled white vinegar
1/4 cup (60 ml) water
1/2 teaspoon (3 ml) salt
Vegetable oil for deep-frying

Sauce
1 heaping teaspoon (6 ml) *sambal badjak*
2 teaspoons (10 ml) smooth peanut butter without
   additives
1/2 teaspoon (3 ml) distilled white vinegar
1/2 teaspoon (3 ml) salt
1 cup (250 ml) coconut milk

Peel the eggplants and slice them crosswise 1/2 inch (1.5 cm) thick. Arrange the slices in a shallow dish. Combine the vinegar, water and salt, stirring well to dissolve the salt, and pour over the eggplant slices. Let stand for 1 hour, then remove the eggplant slices from the solution and pat dry with paper toweling.

Heat oil in a wok or deep pan to a depth of 2 inches (5 cm) until very hot (375°F or 190°C). Deep-fry the eggplant slices, a few at a time, until light brown. Remove with a slotted utensil and drain on paper toweling. To make the sauce, combine all of the ingredients in a saucepan, bring to a gentle boil and simmer, stirring frequently, until sauce thickens slightly. Arrange the eggplant slices in a shallow dish and pour the sauce over them.

SAJOR KERRY
Vegetables in Coconut Milk

1 tablespoon (15 ml) vegetable oil
8 ounces (250 g) lean tender beef, cut into 1-inch
   (3 cm) cubes
1/2 small head cabbage, coarsely cut
3 potatoes, peeled and diced
1 cup (250 ml) coconut milk

Spice mixture
5 kemiri nuts
1 teaspoon (5 ml) ground turmeric
1 teaspoon (5 ml) ground coriander
3 garlic cloves
1 tablespoon (15 ml) chopped onion
1/2 teaspoon (3 ml) ground lemon grass *(sereh)*, or
   1 teaspoon (5 ml) chopped fresh lemon grass
1/2 teaspoon (3 ml) salt
Dried shrimp paste *(trassi)* the size of a peanut

Combine all the ingredients for the spice mixture in a mortar or blender container and blend until smooth. (If using a blender and the motor begins to labor, add some water.) Heat the oil in a Dutch oven, add the spice mixture and stir-fry a few minutes. Add the meat and enough water to cover, bring to a boil, reduce heat, cover and simmer until meat is tender. Add the cabbage and potatoes and continue to simmer until vegetables are tender. Add the coconut milk and heat through. Taste and adjust seasoning with salt before serving.

SAJOR TJAMPOER
Soup with Mixed Vegetables

This soup requires a bit of preparation, but it's so good that it's well worth the effort. Start by purchasing a pork roast with a bone. Ask the butcher to bone the roast, grind at least a half-pound (250 g) of the meat and give all the meat and the bones to you. You'll need the bones for the stock, and the meat you don't use for the soup can be frozen and used at a later date. This soup serves 8 to 10 generously.

Stock
3 quarts (3 L) water
Pork bones
1/2 teaspoon (3 ml) ground nutmeg
2 teaspoons (10 ml) ground ginger
1 teaspoon (5 ml) salt
1 teaspoon (5 ml) ground black pepper
4 garlic cloves, crushed, or
   2 teaspoons (10 ml) garlic powder

Pork and shrimp balls
8 ounces (250 g) ground pork
8 ounces (250 g) small cooked shrimp,
   very finely diced
1 slice stale bread, soaked in a little milk
1 teaspoon (5 ml) salt
1/2 teaspoon (3 ml) garlic powder
1/2 teaspoon (3 ml) ground black pepper

Vegetables
1 cup (250 ml) finely chopped celery leaves
1/2 small head cabbage, finely shredded
1 cup (250 ml) snow peas
4 green onions, thinly sliced

3 tablespoons (45 ml) Indonesian-style soy sauce
   (ketjap)
Juice of 1 small lemon
Freshly cooked long-grain white rice
2 tablespoons (30 ml) French-fried onions

Combine all the ingredients for the stock in a large kettle, bring to a boil, reduce heat, cover and simmer until you have a full-bodied stock, at least 2 to 3 hours. Check the water level and add water if it drops below 3 quarts (3 L). Remove and discard the bones when the stock is ready.

Combine all the ingredients for the pork and shrimp balls, mixing well until it is a nice uniform mixture. Make a test nugget and drop it into the simmering broth. Remove when cooked, taste and adjust salt in the mixture. Form the pork-shrimp mixture into 1-inch (3 cm) balls and add them all at once to the broth. Simmer gently until the balls are cooked through, about 30 to 45 minutes. Now add the vegetables, soy sauce and lemon juice and continuing simmering until the vegetables are tender but still crisp—only a couple of minutes. Taste and adjust seasoning with salt. Ladle over steamed rice and sprinkle with French-fried onions.

Note If you have leftover soup, serve it for lunch the next day with the addition of some boiled Oriental wheat noodles. Omit the rice.

SAJOR LODEH
Vegetables in Coconut Gravy

An old standby. You can use any leftover raw vegetable with the exception of lettuce.

1 tablespoon (15 ml) vegetable oil
1 heaping teaspoon (6 ml) *sambal badjak*
Vegetables: 1 cup (250 ml) green beans; 2 or 3
    carrots, cut into chunks; 1 or 2 zucchini, cut
    into chunks; 1/4 cup (60 ml) green bell pepper
    strips (for a heavenly fragrance); or
    any vegetable combination of choice
2 cups (500 ml) water
1 cup (250 ml) coconut milk

Spice mixture
1 tablespoon (15 ml) chopped onion
4 garlic cloves
4 kemiri nuts
1/2 teaspoon (3 ml) galangal powder *(laos)*
Dried shrimp paste *(trassi)* the size of a peanut
Tamarind pulp *(asem)* the size of 2 peanuts, with
    seeds removed, or
    1/2 teaspoon (3 ml) distilled white vinegar
1 teaspoon (5 ml) sugar
1/2 teaspoon (3 ml) salt

Combine all the ingredients for the spice mixture in a mortar or blender container and blend until smooth. (If using a blender and the motor begins to labor, add a little water.) Set the spice mixture aside. Heat the oil and *sambal badjak* in a Dutch oven. Add the spice mixture and cook a few minutes. Add the vegetables and water, cover and simmer until vegetables are barely tender, about 10 minutes. Add the coconut milk and heat through. Taste and adjust seasoning with salt before serving.

KROEPOEK
Crackers

No self-respecting *rijsttafel* is complete without *kroepoek*. These are crackers made of a number of things, shrimp and fish among them.

Shrimp *kroepoek (kroepoek oedang)* are the most common. Shrimp and flour are pounded into a paste, the paste is shaped into loaves and then the loaves are sliced very thin. The slices are dried in the sun and when very hard, packaged and sold.

This is where we come in. You can buy the shrimp crackers, also commonly called shrimp chips, and deep-fry them in hot oil. Simply heat some oil in a wok or deep pan and drop in a small piece of *kroepoek* to test the temperature. The *kroepoek* should swell within seconds of entering the oil. If the oil is the right temperature proceed, cooking a few of the crackers at a time and lifting them out with a slotted utensil and draining on paper toweling. Be sure that your pan is large enough to accommodate the crackers, since they swell more than twice their size when cooked.

If you've become accustomed to the taste of *kroepoek oedang*, try another flavor. One of the best is *kroepoek blindjoe* or *emping blindjoe*, or sometimes they are simply called *emping*. It is made of the fruit of the blindjoe tree and has a delightful nutlike flavor.

These featherlight crackers can be served with a *rijsttafel* or with drinks. They keep for quite a long time stored in airtight containers.

Seafood

BRENGKESAN
Fish Broiled in Spicy Sauce

1 tablespoon (15 ml) vegetable oil
1 teaspoon (5 ml) *sambal badjak*
1 tablespoon (15 ml) chopped fresh mint leaves
1 pound (500 g) fresh firm-fleshed fish fillets of
   choice

Spice mixture
4 kemiri nuts
1 teaspoon (5 ml) sugar
1 teaspoon (5 ml) distilled white vinegar
1/2 teaspoon (3 ml) salt

To make the spice mixture, combine all the ingredients in a mortar or blender container and blend until smooth. (If using a blender and the motor begins to labor, add a little water.) Heat the oil in a small skillet, add the spice mixture and cook, stirring, until almost dry. Remove from the heat and mix in the *sambal badjak* and mint leaves.

Prepare 3 double thicknesses of aluminum foil large enough to each enclose 2 fish fillets. Place 2 fillets on the center of each piece of foil and cover the fish with the spice mixture. Wrap the foil around the fish and secure closed so that no moisture can escape. Grill over a charcoal fire or set under a broiler about 20 minutes, turning frequently. Open a package slightly and check for doneness before removing from the heat.

PETJEL IKAN
Another Spicy Fish

1 quart (1 L) water
1 teaspoon (5 ml) salt
1 teaspoon (5 ml) distilled white vinegar
6 fresh snapper fillets or fish of choice (about 4
   ounces or 125 g *each*)
Flour (optional)
Vegetable oil for deep-frying
1 cup (250 ml) coconut milk
Salt and sugar to taste
1 heaping teaspoon (7 ml) *sambal badjak*

Combine the water, 1 teaspoon (5 ml) salt and vinegar in a glass or ceramic dish and marinate the fish in the mixture 1 hour. Remove the fish and pat dry with paper toweling. If desired, dredge the fish in flour.

Heat the oil to a depth of about 2 inches (5 cm) until very hot (375°F or 190°C). Deep-fry the fish fillets, 2 at a time, until golden. Remove with a slotted utensil and drain on paper toweling. When all of the fillets are cooked, arrange them in a shallow dish. Combine the coconut milk, salt and sugar to taste, and *sambal badjak* in a small saucepan and place over medium heat. Heat thoroughly, but do not boil. Pour the coconut milk over the fish fillets and serve.

SAMBAL GORENG OEDANG
Shrimp with Snow Peas in Coconut Milk

This is a rather expensive dish, but for a special treat it's worth it.

1-1/2 tablespoons (22 ml) vegetable oil
1 pound (500 g) small cooked shrimp
1 heaping teaspoon (6 ml) *sambal badjak*
A few snips dried citrus leaf *(djeroek poeroet)*
1/2 cup (125 ml) water, or as needed
1 cup (250 ml) snow peas
1 cup (250 ml) coconut milk
1 tablespoon (15 ml) French-fried onions

Spice mixture
1/2 teaspoon (3 ml) galangal powder *(laos)*
3 garlic cloves
Dried shrimp paste *(trassi)* the size of a peanut
1 tablespoon (15 ml) chopped onion
1/2 teaspoon (3 ml) distilled white vinegar
1/2 teaspoon (3 ml) sugar
1/2 teaspoon (3 ml) salt
1/2 teaspoon (3 ml) ground lemon grass *(sereh)*

To make the spice mixture, combine all the ingredients in a mortar or blender container and blend until smooth. (If using a blender and the motor begins to labor, add a little water.) Set the spice mixture aside. Heat the oil in a wok or skillet, add the shrimp and stir-fry about 5 minutes. Add the *sambal badjak,* citrus leaf and spice mixture and mix well. Add the water and snow peas and stir-fry about 2 minutes, or until the peas are almost tender. Add the coconut milk and heat thoroughly, but do not boil. Taste and adjust seasoning with salt. Transfer to a serving dish and sprinkle with French-fried onions.

OEDANG GORENG
Deep-fried Shrimp

Vegetable oil for deep-frying
1-1/2 pounds (750 g) large shrimp, shelled and deveined
Sweet and sour sauce (page 44)

Batter
1/2 cup (125 ml) regular rice flour
1/2 cup (125 ml) water
1 teaspoon (5 ml) garlic powder
1/2 teaspoon (3 ml) salt
1/2 teaspoon (3 ml) ground black pepper

Combine all of the ingredients for the batter and mix well. Heat the oil in a wok or deep pan to a depth of about 2 inches (5 cm) until very hot (375°F or 190°C). Drop the shrimp into the batter, turning them carefully to coat evenly. One at a time, drop the shrimp into the oil, cooking only 3 or 4 at a time. When crispy and golden, remove with a slotted utensil and drain on paper toweling. When all of the shrimp are cooked, serve immediately with the sweet and sour sauce.

KERRIE IKAN
Curried Fish

6 fresh snapper fillets or fish of choice (about
    4 ounces or 125 g *each*)
Flour
Vegetable oil
3 tablespoons (45 ml) chopped onion
1 teaspoon (5 ml) *sambal badjak* (optional)
1-1/2 cups (375 ml) coconut milk
Juice of 1 small lemon

Spice mixture
1-1/2 teaspoons (7 ml) ground coriander
3/4 teaspoon (4 ml) ground cumin
1 teaspoon (5 ml) ground turmeric
1/2 teaspoon (3 ml) ground ginger
4 garlic cloves
1/2 teaspoon (3 ml) ground lemon grass *(sereh)*
Dried shrimp paste *(trassi)* the size of a peanut

Pat the fish fillets dry with paper toweling and
dredge lightly in flour. Heat the oil in a wok or pan
to a depth of 2 inches (5 cm) until very hot (375°F
or 190°C). Deep-fry the fish fillets, 2 at a time,
until golden. Remove with a slotted utensil and
drain on paper toweling; set aside.

Combine all the ingredients for the spice mixture in a mortar or blender container and blend
until smooth. (If using a blender and the motor
begins to labor, add a little water.) Heat 1 tablespoon (15 ml) of the oil in a wok or skillet and
stir-fry the onion, *sambal badjak* and spice mixture
a few minutes until onion is tender. Add the deep-
fried fish fillets and the coconut milk and simmer
gently over low heat, uncovered, until liquid is
reduced by half. Carefully stir in the lemon juice
and serve.

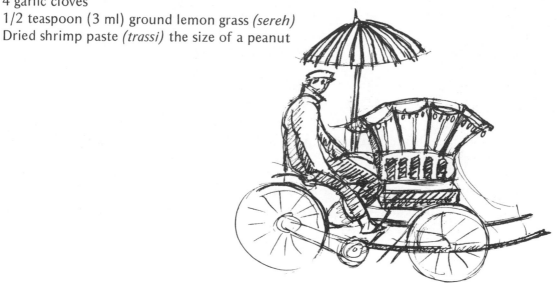

Poultry

SOTO AJAM I
Chicken Soup I

It is said that there are as many versions of *soto ajam* as there are Indonesian cooks. Sharing this soup with family members gives you a nice communal feeling.

1 tablespoon (15 ml) vegetable oil
One 1-1/2- to 2-pound (1 kg) chicken or an equal amount chicken parts
3 quarts (3 L) water
2 tablespoons (30 ml) French-fried onions
2 tablespoons (30 ml) Indonesian-style soy sauce *(ketjap)*
2 tablespoons (30 ml) fresh lemon juice
Freshly cooked long-grain white rice

Spice mixture
3 kemiri nuts
4 garlic cloves
1/2 teaspoon (3 ml) ground coriander
Dried shrimp paste *(trassi)* the size of a peanut
1 teaspoon (5 ml) salt

Garnishes
6 eggs, hard-cooked and cut into quarters
1/2 small head cabbage, coarsely shredded and steamed
3 potatoes, boiled in their jackets, peeled and sliced

Sambal
3 kemiri nuts
3 fresh red chili peppers, seeded, if desired, and diced
Dried shrimp paste *(trassi)* the size of a peanut
1/4 teaspoon (1 to 2 ml) salt

Combine all the ingredients for the spice mixture in a mortar or blender container and blend until smooth. (If using a blender and the motor begins to labor, add some water.) Heat the oil in a 5-quart (5 L) Dutch oven, add the spice mixture and cook, stirring constantly, a few minutes until the spices are pungent. Add the chicken and water, bring to a boil, reduce heat, cover and simmer gently about 50 or 60 minutes, or until chicken is tender. Remove the chicken from the broth and skin and bone it. Cut the meat into small pieces and put it back in the pot along with the French-fried onions, soy sauce and lemon juice. Taste and adjust seasoning with salt.

While the soup is cooking, prepare the garnishes and put them in separate bowls on the table. Prepare the *sambal* by grinding all of the ingredients together in a mortar. Transfer it to a small bowl and set it on the table with the garnishes. To serve, each diner spoons rice into the bottom of his bowl, ladles the boiling soup over the top and adds garnishes and *sambal* according to taste.

SOTO AJAM II
Chicken Soup II

A more delicate version of this popular soup.

One 1-1/2- to 2-pound (1 kg) chicken or an equal
    amount chicken parts
3 quarts (3 L) water
1 tablespoon (15 ml) vegetable oil
2 tablespoons (30 ml) Indonesian-style soy sauce
    (ketjap)
1 tablespoon (15 ml) fresh lemon juice
1 cup (250 ml) thinly sliced celery
3 or 4 leeks, thinly sliced (optional)
2 tablespoons (30 ml) French-fried onions
Freshly cooked long-grain white rice

Spice mixture
3 garlic cloves
1-1/2 teaspoons (7 ml) ground ginger, or
    2 slices ginger root
1 teaspoon (5 ml) salt
1 teaspoon (5 ml) ground turmeric

Garnishes and sambal as for Soto Ajam I
    (page 29)

Put the chicken in a 5-quart (5 L) Dutch oven with
the water and bring to a boil. Reduce heat, cover
and simmer until tender, about 50 or 60 minutes.
Remove the chicken from the broth, reserve
the broth in the pot and skin and bone the chick-
en. Cut the meat into small pieces and return it to
the pot.

    Combine all the ingredients for the spice mix-
ture in a mortar or blender container and blend
until smooth. (If using a blender and the motor
begins to labor, add some water.) Heat the oil in a
small pan, add the spice mixture and cook, stirring,
until the spices are pungent. Add the spices to the
broth and chicken meat, bring to a boil, reduce
heat, cover and simmer about 30 minutes. Add the
soy sauce, lemon juice, celery, leeks and French-
fried onions and simmer until the vegetables are
tender but still crisp.

    While the soup is cooking, prepare the gar-
nishes and *sambal*. Serve the soup as directed in
Soto Ajam I.

AJAM KETJAP
Grilled Chicken in Soy Sauce

Two 2-pound (1 kg *each*) chickens, cut into quar-
    ters, or 4 chicken drumsticks and thighs and
    2 chicken breasts

Marinade
1 cup (250 ml) Indonesian-style soy sauce
    (ketjap)
Juice of 1 medium lemon
3 garlic cloves, crushed
1 tablespoon (15 ml) vegetable oil
Dash sugar

Put the chicken into a glass or ceramic bowl. Combine all the ingredients for the marinade and pour
over the chicken, turning to coat evenly. Marinate
overnight, refrigerated. Grill the chicken pieces
over a charcoal fire or broil under a broiler until
golden and tender, basting frequently with the
leftover marinade.

AJAM BOEMBOE OPOR
Chicken with Coconut Milk

3/4 cup (175 ml) vegetable oil
4 chicken drumsticks and thighs and 2 chicken
  breasts
A few snips dried citrus leaf *(djeroek poeroet)*
1 bay leaf
1 teaspoon (5 ml) distilled white vinegar
Chicken stock or water
1 cup (250 ml) coconut milk

Spice mixture
2 tablespoons (30 ml) chopped onion
4 garlic cloves
5 kemiri nuts
Dried shrimp paste *(trassi)* the size of a large
  peanut
1/2 teaspoon (3 ml) galangal powder *(laos)*
1/2 teaspoon (3 ml) ground lemon grass *(sereh)*
1 teaspoon (5 ml) ground coriander
1/2 teaspoon (3 ml) ground cumin
1/2 teaspoon (3 ml) sugar
1/2 teaspoon (3 ml) salt

Heat the oil in a Dutch oven, add the chicken pieces and brown on all sides. While the chicken is browning, combine all the ingredients for the spice mixture in a mortar or blender container and blend until smooth. (If using a blender and the motor begins to labor, add a little of the chicken stock or water.) Pour any excess oil off of the chicken and add the spice mixture, citrus leaf, bay leaf, vinegar and enough chicken stock or water to just cover. Cook over medium heat, covered, until the chicken is tender. Add the coconut milk and heat gently until warmed through. Taste and adjust seasoning with salt before serving.

PETJEL AJAM
Spicy Chicken

3/4 cup (175 ml) vegetable oil
4 chicken drumsticks and thighs and 2 chicken
  breasts
1 teaspoon (5 ml) *sambal badjak*
1 cup (250 ml) coconut milk
1 tablespoon (15 ml) chopped fresh mint leaves

Spice mixture
3 garlic cloves
Dried shrimp paste *(trassi)* the size of a peanut
1/2 teaspoon (3 ml) ground aromatic ginger
  (kentjoer)
1/2 teaspoon (3 ml) sugar
1/2 teaspoon (3 ml) salt
1 teaspoon (5 ml) fresh lemon juice

Heat the oil in a Dutch oven, add the chicken pieces, and cook until tender and browned. While the chicken is cooking, combine all the ingredients for the spice mixture in a mortar or blender container and blend until smooth. (If using a blender and the motor begins to labor, add a little water.) Stir the *sambal badjak* and coconut milk into the spice mixture. Pour any excess oil off of the chicken and add the coconut milk mixture. Heat gently until warmed through. Taste and adjust seasoning with salt. Transfer to a serving dish and garnish with mint leaves.

AJAM BOEMBOE ROEDJAK
Pepper Chicken

3/4 cup (175 ml) vegetable oil
2 fryer chickens, cut into serving pieces
2 cups (500 ml) coconut milk
A few snips dried citrus leaf *(djeroek poeroet)*

Spice mixture
1 medium onion, chopped
5 garlic cloves
2 teaspoons (10 ml) *sambal badjak*
5 kemiri nuts, or
   1-1/2 teaspoons (7 ml) crunchy-style peanut
   butter without additives
Dried shrimp paste *(trassi)* the size of a peanut
1 teaspoon (5 ml) distilled white vinegar
1 teaspoon (5 ml) sugar
1 teaspoon (5 ml) salt

Heat the oil in a wok or skillet and brown the
chicken pieces well on all sides. While the chicken
is browning, combine all the ingredients for the
spice mixture in a mortar or blender container and
blend until smooth. (If using a blender and the
motor begins to labor, add a little water.) Combine
the coconut milk, citrus leaf and spice mixture in a
saucepan and bring just to a simmer. Add the
browned chicken pieces and simmer gently, bath-
ing the chicken with the sauce. Cook, uncovered,
until the liquid is reduced by half. This dish will
serve 8 persons.

RISSOLES
"Piggies in a Blanket"

Though this recipe involves a bit of work, if you
decide to try it you're in for a very special treat.
Served with a simple green salad, rissoles make a
fancy lunch. Add a nice soup and you have an
excellent light supper. You may substitute your
own favorite crêpe recipe for the one given here.

Filling
2 tablespoons (30 ml) butter
3 tablespoons (45 ml) finely chopped onion
3 tablespoons (45 ml) finely chopped celery
1 teaspoon (5 ml) salt
1 teaspoon (5 ml) sugar
1/2 teaspoon (3 ml) ground nutmeg
1/2 teaspoon (3 ml) ground ginger
1/2 teaspoon (3 ml) ground black pepper
1-1/2 pounds (750 g) meaty chicken parts (or a
   small chicken), boiled in water to cover until
   tender, boned, skinned and meat very finely
   diced
1 teaspoon (5 ml) dry onion soup mix (optional)
1-1/2 cups (375 ml) chicken stock
3 tablespoons (45 ml) dry sherry
Juice of 1/2 lemon
1/2 cup (125 ml) all-purpose flour
1/2 cup (125 ml) milk
2 eggs, beaten

Crêpes
4 eggs, at room temperature
2 cups (500 ml) milk
1 cup (250 ml) water
3 cups (750 ml) all-purpose flour
4 tablespoons (60 ml) vegetable oil
1/8 teaspoon (scant 1 ml) salt
Butter

3 egg whites, beaten foamy, or
   canned evaporated milk
Dry bread crumbs
Vegetable oil for deep-frying

To make the filling, melt the butter in a saucepan, add the onion, celery, salt, sugar, nutmeg, ginger and pepper; sauté until onion is translucent. Add chicken and mix in well. At this point you can add the optional onion soup mix. It gives the filling a pleasant piquant flavor. Now add the chicken stock, sherry and lemon juice and simmer very gently a minute or two. Mix together the flour, milk and eggs until you have a smooth paste and blend it into the chicken. Cook, stirring, until thick and bubbly. Remove from the heat and let cool before filling the crêpes.

To make the crêpes, beat the eggs lightly. Mix together the milk and water and alternately add this mixture and the flour to the eggs, beating well after each addition. Add the oil and salt and beat again. The batter must be smooth. Let stand at least 1 hour (or as long as overnight). Heat about 1 teaspoon (5 ml) butter in a 7- or 8-inch (18 or 20 cm) omelet pan or skillet with sloping sides over medium heat. Pour about 4 tablespoons (50 ml) of the batter into the pan and lift and tilt the pan so that the batter evenly covers the bottom surface. Cook only until the crêpe becomes dry on top, about 1 minute, then slide the crêpe out onto a plate. Repeat with remaining batter, adding butter to the pan as needed. Stack the crêpes as they are cooked; you should have about 30 in all.

Spoon a very generous tablespoon (20 ml) of the chicken mixture on the lower one third of each crêpe. Fold the lower edge over the filling, fold in the sides and then fold over the far edge, forming an envelope shape. Heat oil in a wok or deep pan to a depth of about 2 inches (5 cm) until very hot (375°F or 190°C). Coat each rissole with egg white or evaporated milk and then roll in the bread crumbs. Deep-fry the rissoles, 3 or 4 at a time, until golden. Remove with a slotted utensil and drain on paper toweling. Serve hot.

Beef & Pork

BOEMBOE BALI
Spicy Beef

1-1/2-pound-piece (750 g) lean tender beef
3 tablespoons (45 ml) vegetable oil
1/4 cup (60 ml) Indonesian-style soy sauce
  (ketjap)
1 teaspoon (5 ml) sugar

Spice mixture
1 heaping teaspoon (7 ml) *sambal badjak*
1 teaspoon (5 ml) ground ginger
5 garlic cloves
Dried shrimp paste *(trassi)* the size of a peanut
Juice of 1 small lemon
1/2 teaspoon (2 ml) salt

Put the beef in a saucepan with water to cover and simmer until cooked but still firm. While the beef is cooking, combine all of the ingredients for the spice mixture in a mortar or blender container and blend until smooth; set aside. Remove the beef from its cooking water, drain well and cut into 1/2-inch-thick (1.5 cm) slices. Heat the oil in a wok or skillet, add the beef and stir-fry about 10 minutes. Remove the beef from the pan with a slotted utensil and set aside. Add the spice mixture and stir-fry a few minutes. Return the meat to the pan, add the soy sauce and sugar and enough water to barely cover the meat. Bring to a boil, then simmer until the liquid reduces by half. Taste and adjust seasoning with salt.

HACHE
Hash

3 tablespoons (45 ml) vegetable oil
2-1/2 pounds (1.25 kg) lean tender beef, cut into
  1-inch (3 cm) cubes
2 medium onions, sliced
2 garlic cloves, crushed
1/2 teaspoon (3 ml) ground nutmeg
1/4 teaspoon (1 to 2 ml) ground cloves
1 teaspoon (5 ml) sugar
1 teaspoon (5 ml) salt
1 teaspoon (5 ml) distilled white vinegar
3 tablespoons (45 ml) Indonesian-style soy
  sauce *(ketjap)*
3 medium potatoes, peeled and thickly sliced
3 or 4 leeks, diced

Heat the oil in a wok or Dutch oven and brown the beef cubes on all sides. Add the onions, garlic, nutmeg, cloves, sugar, salt and vinegar and cook, stirring constantly, about 5 minutes. Add the soy sauce and enough water to barely cover the meat. Bring to a boil, reduce heat, cover and simmer until beef is almost done, about 45 minutes. Add the potatoes and leeks and continue to simmer, covered, until the vegetables are very tender. Taste and adjust seasoning with salt.

BEBOTOK
Steamed Meatloaf

2 pounds (1 kg) ground lean beef
3 eggs, beaten
1 cup (250 ml) coconut milk, or as needed

Spice mixture
3 tablespoons (45 ml) chopped onion
5 garlic cloves
1 teaspoon (5 ml) ground coriander
1/2 teaspoon (3 ml) ground cumin
1/2 teaspoon (3 ml) galangal powder *(laos)*
Dried shrimp paste *(trassi)* the size of a peanut
2 fresh small red chili peppers, seeded
1 teaspoon (5 ml) salt

Combine all the ingredients for the spice mixture in a mortar or blender container and blend until smooth. (If using a blender and the motor begins to labor, add a little water.) Mix together the ground beef, eggs, coconut milk and spice mixture until well blended. If the mixture seems too stiff, add a little more coconut milk.

Bring a small amount of water to a boil in a saucepan and drop in a test nugget of the beef mixture to cook. Taste and adjust seasoning with salt. Pack the beef mixture into a 6-cup (1.5 L) steamed pudding mold or a 1-pound (500 g) coffee can with the top removed. Bring some water to a boil in a deep stockpot. Put the pudding mold or the coffee can into the pot. The water should reach about halfway up the side of the mold or coffee can. Cover the pot and steam over medium heat until the meat mixture appears very pale in color, about 1-1/4 to 1-1/2 hours. Pierce with a knife to check for doneness. The water level should remain constant throughout the cooking period, so check the pot from time to time. When the meatloaf is ready, remove it from the pot and run a sharp knife around the edge to loosen it. Slide the loaf out onto a platter and slice to serve.

FRIKADEL
Meatloaf

Though the name is Dutch, the seasonings are strictly Indonesian.

1-1/2 pounds (750 g) ground lean pork
1-1/2 pounds (750 g) ground lean beef
3 slices white bread, soaked in a little milk,
    squeezed dry and shredded, or
    2 medium potatoes, boiled in their jackets,
    peeled and mashed
4 eggs, beaten
1/2 teaspoon (3 ml) ground cloves
1 teaspoon (5 ml) ground nutmeg
1/2 teaspoon (3 ml) ground black pepper
1/2 teaspoon (3 ml) garlic powder
2 green onions, finely sliced
1 cup (250 ml) beef stock
About 1/2 cup (125 ml) dry bread crumbs

Combine the pork, beef, bread or potatoes, eggs, cloves, nutmeg, black pepper, garlic powder and green onions, mixing well. Pack the mixture into a shallow casserole and pour the beef stock over it. Sprinkle with the bread crumbs and bake in a preheated 350°F (180°C) oven about 1-1/2 hours, or until done.

ABON
"Monkey Hair"

This rather curious preparation is typical of a number of strongly flavored dishes prepared by Indonesians for eating in small amounts with bland rice. Though beef is used here, similar dishes, colloquially called "rice pullers," are made with prawns and fish. Dishes like this one and Sambal Goreng Kering (page 38) are, because of the absence of liquid, almost nonperishable. They will keep for months in airtight containers and are necessary parts of a good *rijsttafel*.

One 2-1/2-pound (1.25 kg) lean boneless beef roast
1/2 cup (125 ml) vegetable oil
1 cup (250 ml) coconut milk
Fresh red chili peppers, seeded and cut into
   matchstick strips
Vegetable oil for deep-frying

Spice mixture
2 small onions, chopped
5 garlic cloves
2 teaspoons (10 ml) ground coriander
1 teaspoon (5 ml) ground cumin
1/2 teaspoon (3 ml) ground turmeric
1/2 teaspoon (3 ml) ground black pepper
Dried shrimp paste *(trassi)* the size of a peanut
1/2 teaspoon (3 ml) ground lemon grass *(sereh)*
1/2 teaspoon (3 ml) galangal powder *(laos)*
1-1/2 teaspoons (7 ml) distilled white vinegar
1-1/2 teaspoons (7 ml) sugar
1 teaspoon (5 ml) salt

Put the meat in a pan with water to cover, bring to a boil, reduce heat, and simmer until the meat is very tender and separates easily when pulled with a spoon, about 1-1/2 hours. Drain the meat very well and discard any visible fat. Grate the meat in *very small* amounts in a blender (if you attempt too much at once, the meat will form a paste) or in a food processor fitted with the meat blade. If these methods are not possible, put the meat on a cutting board and pound it with a meat mallet until it forms shreds. (This is hard work and time-consuming.) Set the meat aside.

Combine all the ingredients for the spice mixture in a mortar or blender container and blend until smooth. Heat the oil in a wok or skillet and stir-fry the spice mixture for a few minutes. Add the meat and coconut milk and continue stir-frying 10 minutes. Place the wok in a preheated 300°F (150°C) oven until the mixture is very dry and crumbly, about 3 hours, stirring regularly.

While the meat is in the oven, heat oil to a depth of about 1 inch (3 cm) in a wok or skillet. Put the matchstick-cut chili peppers in a wire strainer and immerse in the hot oil for a few seconds, then drain on paper toweling. Serve the meat with the chili peppers sprinkled over it. The *abon* can be stored in airtight containers for several months.

SAMBAL GORENG KERING
Fried Beef and Pepper Strips

1-pound-piece (500 g) lean tender beef
3 tablespoons (45 ml) vegetable oil, or as needed
2 fresh long red chili peppers, seeded and cut
   into matchstick
1 tablespoon (15 ml) French-fried onions

Spice mixture
3 garlic cloves
1/2 teaspoon (3 ml) galangal powder *(laos)*
Dried shrimp paste *(trassi)* the size of a peanut
1 teaspoon (5 ml) sugar
1 teaspoon (5 ml) distilled white vinegar
1 scant teaspoon (4 ml) salt

Put the beef in a saucepan with water to cover and simmer until cooked but still firm. Drain well and remove all visible fat. Slice the beef into strips slightly larger than shoestring-potato size. Heat the oil in a wok or skillet and stir-fry the beef strips until browned. Remove with a slotted utensil and set aside. Heat the oil in the wok, adding more if necessary, add the pepper strips and stir-fry until browned. Remove with a slotted utensil and set aside. Pour off all but 1 tablespoon (15 ml) of the oil in the pan. Combine all the ingredients for the spice mixture in a mortar or blender container and blend until smooth. (If using a blender and the motor begins to labor, add a little water.) Heat the oil remaining in the pan, add the spice mixture and stir-fry a few minutes. Return the beef and pepper strips to the pan, add the fried onions and mix just until well combined.

Variations French-fried potatoes or *tempeh*(whole-soybean cakes) strips may be substituted for the beef. Peel and cut 1 pound (500 g) of potatoes as you would for French-fried potatoes. (If you have a food processor, the cutting will be a snap.) Deep-fry the potatoes and drain on paper toweling. Beginning with the browning of the chili pepper strips, proceed as directed in the above recipe.

If using *tempeh,* cut the cakes into shoestring-sized strips. Deep-fry the strips in oil and drain on paper toweling. Beginning with the browning of the chili pepper strips, proceed as directed in the above recipe.

SATE KOENING
Barbecued Beef with Turmeric

In Indonesia, tough cuts of meat are wrapped in papaya leaves for a few hours before cooking. The enzymes that occur naturally in the leaves act as a tenderizer.

2 pounds (1 kg) tender lean beef, cut into 1-inch
   (3 cm) cubes
1 cup (250 ml) coconut milk

Spice mixture
5 kemiri nuts
1 teaspoon (5 ml) ground coriander
1/2 teaspoon (3 ml) ground cumin
1 teaspoon (5 ml) galangal powder *(laos)*
1 teaspoon (5 ml) ground turmeric
1 teaspoon (5 ml) brown sugar
1 teaspoon (5 ml) salt
1 teaspoon (5 ml) fresh lemon juice
1/2 teaspoon (3 ml) *sambal badjak*
4 garlic cloves
1-1/2 tablespoons (22 ml) chopped onion

Combine all the ingredients for the spice mixture in a mortar or blender container and blend until smooth. (If using a blender and the motor begins to labor, add a little water.) Pour the coconut milk into the blended spice mixture and mix gently. Put the beef cubes in a glass or ceramic dish and pour the coconut milk mixture over them. Marinate for a few hours, refrigerated. Thread the beef cubes on 10 to 12 10-inch (25 cm) metal skewers and grill over a charcoal fire until well browned on all sides. Baste the beef cubes with the remaining marinade as they cook.

PASTEI GALIGNY
Meat Pastries

Pastry dough
2 eggs
2 cups (500 ml) unbleached flour
1/4 teaspoon (1 to 2 ml) salt
6 tablespoons (90 ml) butter, at room temperature
Scant 1/4 cup (50 ml) water

About 1-1/2 cups (375 ml) Abon (page 37)
3 or 4 eggs, hard-cooked and sliced
Vegetable oil for deep-frying
Sharp prepared mustard

To make the pastry dough, beat the eggs in a large bowl and then work in the flour, salt, butter and water, mixing well until the mixture forms a ball. The dough should be firm. Let the dough rest in a cool place 1 hour.

Divide the dough into 2 or 3 portions, depending on how large your work surface is, and roll out a portion at a time to the thickness of a silver dollar. Cut out rounds 4 inches (10 cm) in diameter (a 1-pound or 500-g coffee can works well). Put about 1 teaspoon (5 ml) of the *abon* in the center of each round and top with a hard-cooked egg slice. Moisten the edges of the round with water and fold in half to form a half-moon shape. Press the edges with the tines of a fork to seal.

Heat oil in a wok or skillet to a depth of about 2 inches (5 cm) until very hot (about 375°F or 190°C). Drop 2 or 3 of the pastries into the hot oil at a time and fry until golden brown. Serve hot with sharp mustard.

Note If you have a food processor, the pastry dough is easy to prepare. Put all the ingredients into the processor bowl at once, and using the meat or pastry blade, process until the mixture forms a ball.

Variation Substitute the creamed chicken used for Rissoles (page 32) for the beef filling. Proceed as directed in the recipe.

FRIKADEL LOMBOK
Stuffed Red Peppers

12 fresh long red chili peppers
Vegetable oil for deep-frying

Filling
1 pound (500 g) ground lean beef
2 medium potatoes, boiled in their jackets, peeled
   and mashed
2 eggs, beaten
1/2 teaspoon (3 ml) ground black pepper
1/2 teaspoon (3 ml) salt
2 green onions, finely sliced

To make the filling, combine all the ingredients and mix well. Cook a test nugget of the mixture until golden in some of the oil. Taste and adjust seasoning with salt; set the filling aside.

Make a lengthwise slit in each chili pepper, taking care not to disturb the stem end. Remove the seeds and membranes and stuff each pepper with an equal portion of the filling. (You may want to wear rubber gloves when removing the seeds to protect your hands from the peppers' volatile oils.) The peppers will resemble boats with a slight mound in the middle.

Heat oil in a wok or deep pan to a depth of 2 inches (5 cm) until very hot (about 375°F or 190°C). Carefully drop the peppers into the oil, 2 or 3 at a time, and cook until golden brown. Remove from the oil with a slotted utensil and drain on paper toweling. Keep the peppers warm until all are cooked, then arrange in a shallow dish to serve.

REMPAH
French-fried Beef-Coconut Balls

Delicious with rice or alone as a snack.

8 ounces (250 g) ground lean beef
1 cup (250 ml) unsweetened dried grated coconut,
   mixed with 1/2 cup (125 ml) water
2 dried citrus leaves *(djeroek poeroet),* very finely
   shredded
2 eggs, beaten
Vegetable oil for deep-frying

Spice mixture
3 kemiri nuts
Dried shrimp paste *(trassi)* the size of a peanut
3 tablespoons (45 ml) chopped onion
3 garlic cloves
1/2 teaspoon (3 ml) galangal powder *(laos)*
1 teaspoon (5 ml) ground coriander
1/2 teaspoon (3 ml) ground cumin
1/2 teaspoon (3 ml) salt
1 teaspoon (5 ml) sugar
1 teaspoon (5 ml) distilled white vinegar
1 teaspoon (5 ml) *sambal badjak* (optional)

Combine all the ingredients for the spice mixture in a mortar or blender container and blend until smooth. Mix together the ground beef, coconut and water, citrus leaves, eggs and spice mixture until smooth and the spices are well distributed.

Heat oil in a wok or deep pan to a depth of 2 inches (5 cm) until very hot (about 375°F or

190°C). Make a test nugget of the beef mixture, drop into the hot oil and fry until golden. Taste and adjust seasoning with salt. Form the beef mixture into 1-inch (3 cm) balls and drop them into the oil, adding only enough at a time so that they are not crowded. Cook until golden brown and crisp. Drain on paper toweling and serve.

SATE GURI
Savory Barbecued Beef on Skewers

2-1/2 pounds (1.25 kg) lean tender beef, cut into
    1-inch (3 cm) cubes
Saus Kacang (page 42)

Marinade
4 garlic cloves
2 tablespoons (30 ml) Indonesian-style soy sauce
    (ketjap)
1 tablespoon (15 ml) fresh lemon juice
1 tablespoon (15 ml) brown sugar
1/2 teaspoon (2 ml) salt
1 cup (250 ml) coconut milk

Put the beef cubes in a glass or ceramic bowl. Combine all the ingredients for the marinade in a blender container and blend until well mixed. Pour the marinade over the beef cubes, turning them to coat evenly, and marinate for at least 1 hour, refrigerated. Thread the meat on 12 10-inch (25 cm) metal skewers and grill over a charcoal fire, turning the skewers continuously and basting with the remaining marinade, until the beef is cooked. Serve with Saus Kacang on the side.

SATE BABI
Barbecued Pork on Skewers

2-1/2 pounds (1.25 kg) lean tender pork, cut into
  1-inch (3 cm) cubes
Saus Kacang (following recipe)

Marinade
1/2 cup (125 ml) Indonesian-style soy sauce
  (ketjap)
1-1/2 teaspoons (7 ml) ground coriander
1/2 teaspoon (3 ml) ground cumin
4 garlic cloves
1 teaspoon (5 ml) brown sugar
1/2 teaspoon (3 ml) salt

Put the pork cubes in a glass or ceramic bowl.
Combine all of the ingredients for the marinade in
a blender container and blend until well mixed.
Pour the marinade over the pork cubes, turning
them to coat evenly, and marinate for at least 1
hour, refrigerated. Thread the meat on 12 10-inch
(25 cm) metal skewers and grill over a charcoal
fire, turning the skewers continuously and basting
with the remaining marinade, until the pork is
cooked. Serve with Saus Kacang on the side.

SAUS KACANG
Peanut Sauce

3 heaping tablespoons (55 ml) crunchy-style
  peanut butter without additives
1-1/2 teaspoons (7 ml) shrimp sauce *(petis)*
1 teaspoon (5 ml) *sambal badjak*
1 teaspoon (5 ml) sugar
1/2 teaspoon (2 ml) salt
2 cups (500 ml) water
1/2 cup (125 ml) coconut milk

Mix together peanut butter, shrimp sauce, *sambal
badjak*, sugar and salt in a medium saucepan. Stir
until the ingredients are well incorporated and then
gradually stir in the water. Place the pan over high
heat and bring to a boil, stirring constantly. Reduce the heat so the sauce just simmers and cook,
stirring often, until reduced to about 1-1/2 cups
(375 ml). Add the coconut milk and simmer about
30 minutes longer. If the sauce is too thick, add a
little water to thin it.

BABI KETJAP
Pork Simmered in Soy Sauce

The influence of the Chinese on Indonesian cooking is apparent in this and the following recipes' use of pork. Though the majority of Indonesia's population are practicing Muslims, a faith that proscribes the eating of pork, for those who are not, pork is a popular meat.

2 tablespoons (30 ml) vegetable oil
3 pounds (1.5 kg) tender lean pork, cut into
    1-inch (3 cm) cubes
Salt to taste

Spice mixture
5 slices ginger root, or
    2 teaspoons (10 ml) ground ginger
5 garlic cloves
1 teaspoon (5 ml) brown sugar
1/2 cup (125 ml) Indonesian-style soy sauce
    (ketjap)

Heat the oil in a wok or Dutch oven, add the pork cubes and cook until browned on all sides. While the meat is cooking, combine all the ingredients for the spice mixture in a blender container and blend until smooth. When the meat is browned, pour off all but 1 tablespoon (15 ml) of the oil in the pan. Add the spice mixture and enough water to just cover the pork and bring to a boil. Reduce the heat and simmer, covered, until meat is tender, about 45 minutes. If too much of the liquid cooks away, add a little water. Taste and adjust seasoning with salt before serving.

BABI TAOTJO
Pork in Soybean Sauce

2 tablespoons (30 ml) vegetable oil
2 pounds (1 kg) tender lean pork, cut into 1-inch
    (3 cm) cubes
1 cup (250 ml) soybean condiment*
3 tablespoons (45 ml) Indonesian-style soy sauce
    (ketjap)
1 cup (250 ml) finely sliced leeks or green onions
Salt to taste

Spice mixture
2 small onions, chopped
4 garlic cloves
1 teaspoon (5 ml) ground ginger
1/2 teaspoon (3 ml) ground black pepper

Heat the oil in a wok or Dutch oven and brown the pork cubes on all sides. While the meat is browning, combine all the ingredients for the spice mixture in a mortar or blender container and blend until smooth. (If using a blender and the motor begins to labor, add a little water.) Add the spice mixture to the meat and cook, stirring, a few minutes. Then add the soybean condiment, soy sauce and enough water to just cover the meat and simmer, covered, until the pork is tender, about 45 minutes. Add the leeks or green onions and mix well through the meat. Taste and adjust seasoning with salt.

*Soybean condiment is available in jars and cans at Chinese and other Oriental markets and some supermarkets. The Chinese product, suitable for use in this recipe, is variously called brown bean sauce and bean sauce.

PANGSIET
Won tons with Sweet and Sour Sauce

1-pound (500 g) package square won ton skins
Vegetable oil for deep-frying

Filling
1 pound (500 g) ground lean pork
1 teaspoon (5 ml) ground ginger
1 teaspoon (5 ml) salt
1 teaspoon (5 ml) garlic powder
1/2 teaspoon (3 ml) ground black pepper

Sweet and sour sauce
3/4 cup (200 ml) puréed tomatoes
1 cup (250 ml) water
1/2 teaspoon (3 ml) salt
1 tablespoon (15 ml) sugar
2 teaspoons (10 ml) distilled white vinegar
1 teaspoon (5 ml) ground ginger
1 teaspoon (5 ml) garlic powder
1 teaspoon (5 ml) hot prepared mustard

To make the filling, stir-fry the pork over medium heat until it loses its pink color. Drain off any fat and transfer the cooked meat to a bowl. Mix in the ginger, salt, garlic powder and black pepper.

Have a cookie sheet, board or anything flat ready to put the won tons on after they have been filled and a small bowl of water at hand. Put a won ton wrapper in the palm of your left hand, dip the fingers of your right hand in the water and quickly and lightly moisten the surface of the wrapper. Put 1 teaspoon (5 ml) of the filling in the middle of the wrapper and fold the wrapper into a triangle, pressing the edges together. Then pinch the two ends of the long side of the triangle together, dabbing them with a little water if necessary to seal them. (You will of course reverse the left-and-right-hand orientation if you are left-handed.)

When all of the won tons have been filled, heat oil in a wok or deep pan to a depth of about 2 inches (5 cm) until very hot (375°F or 190°C). Deep-fry the won tons a few at a time until golden. Remove with a slotted utensil and drain on paper toweling.

Prepare the sweet and sour sauce while deep-frying the won tons. Combine all the ingredients in a saucepan, bring to a boil, reduce heat and simmer about 10 minutes, stirring occasionally. Serve the won tons hot with the sauce on the side.

Sweets

KWEE TALAM
Brown and White Pudding

Brown layer
1/2 pack hardened brown sugar*
1/4 cup (60 ml) water
1 cup (250 ml) coconut milk
1/4 cup (60 ml) regular rice flour
1/4 cup (60 ml) cornstarch
1/4 teaspoon (1 ml) salt

White layer
1 cup (250 ml) coconut milk
3 tablespoons (45 ml) regular rice flour
Pinch salt

To make the brown layer, combine the brown sugar and water in a saucepan placed over low heat and heat until the sugar is melted. Strain the liquified sugar and return to the saucepan. Combine the rice flour and cornstarch and add a little of the coconut milk to it to form a paste. Add this mixture to the sugar along with the salt and bring slowly to a boil, stirring constantly. When the mixture is thick and bubbly, pour it into a 9-inch (23 cm) cake pan, spreading it to the edges of the pan with a spatula and smoothing out the surface. Set aside.

To make the white layer, combine all of the ingredients in a saucepan and cook slowly over medium heat until it bubbles, stirring constantly. Pour the mixture over the brown layer, spreading it to the edges with a spatula and smoothing out the surface. Let cool completely and cut into wedges to serve.

*This hardened brown sugar is made in the Philippines and is sold in packages weighing about 1-1/2 pounds (750 g). The sugar is formed in half-dome-shaped molds and wrapped in pandanus leaves. Remove the leaves before putting the sugar in the saucepan. The sugar is strained after liquifying to remove bits of the leaves that may remain.

PISANG GORENG
Banana Fritters

There is no tree in Indonesia that has as many uses as the banana tree. As children, we loved to sneak out to a little roadside foodstand to buy rice, freshly cooked in a banana leaf wrapper; the leaves gave the rice delicious fragrance. The flowers are steamed and eaten as a vegetable. The fruit is eaten fresh, made into fritters or sliced and dried for chips or to be made into flour. And when one gets caught in a sudden downpour, the huge leaf makes an excellent umbrella.

1 cup (250 ml) all-purpose flour
2 tablespoons (30 ml) sugar
1/4 cup (60 ml) water
1 egg, beaten
1/4 teaspoon (2 ml) salt
4 or 5 large ripe bananas
Vegetable oil for deep-frying
Sugar

Mix together the flour, sugar, water, egg and salt to make a smooth batter. If the batter seems a little heavy, add a little more water. Peel the bananas and cut them in half lengthwise, then cut each half in 2 or 3 pieces. Add the banana pieces to the batter and mix gently, taking care that the pieces are evenly coated with the batter. Heat the oil to a depth of about 2 inches (5 cm) in a wok or deep saucepan until very hot (375°F or 190°C). Drop in the banana pieces, a few at a time, and brown evenly on all sides. Remove with a slotted utensil and drain on paper toweling. Serve warm, dusted with sugar.

APEM
Little Yeast Pancake

You will need to purchase a coconut to make this recipe, as it uses the liquid in the nut.

1 cup (250 ml) coconut liquid (add water, if necessary, to make measure)
2 teaspoons (10 ml) active dry yeast
1-1/2 cups (375 ml) regular rice flour
1 cup (250 ml) sugar
2 eggs, beaten
1/4 teaspoon (2 ml) salt
1 cup (250 ml) coconut milk
Vegetable oil
Melted butter and sugar

Heat the coconut liquid to lukewarm and dissolve the yeast in it. Mix together the coconut liquid-yeast mixture, rice flour, sugar, eggs and salt to make a smooth batter. Set aside in a warm place and let rise overnight. The next morning, carefully mix in the coconut milk.

Heat a small amount of oil in a wok or skillet over medium heat. Drop in about 1-1/2 table-spoons (22 ml) batter, and when it becomes some-what solid on top, press down the middle with a spatula and then turn it over. When little bubbles appear and the edges turn dark, remove and keep warm. Repeat with remaining batter, adding oil as needed. Serve drizzled with melted butter and dusted with sugar.

ROTI KOEKOES
Steamed Bread

2 cups (500 ml) super-fine sugar, sifted
6 large eggs
1 teaspoon (5 ml) vanilla extract, or
　1 vanilla bean*
2 cups (500 ml) all-purpose flour
1/2 teaspoon (3 ml) baking powder
Confectioners' sugar and melted butter

Beat together the sugar and eggs until very light in color. (An electric mixer makes this job easy.) Mix in the vanilla extract or bean. Gradually add the flour and baking powder, mixing in well.

　Bring water to a boil in your steaming unit. Line the container that will hold the bread (either the top pan of a double-pan steamer or a dish set in an improvised steamer (see page 150) with a triple thickness of cheesecloth. If your steamer is 3 quart (3 L) or larger, you can steam the batter all at once. If not, halve the batter and steam half at a time. Pour the batter into the cheesecloth, cover the steamer and steam until a wooden pick inserted in the center comes out clean, about 1 hour and 15 minutes. Check from time to time to make sure the water level remains constant. When the bread is ready, grab the corners of the cheesecloth and lift the bread from the steamer. Turn the bread, face down, onto a plate that has been sprinkled with confectioners' sugar. Drizzle with butter and serve sliced into wedges.

*If you are using a vanilla bean, hold the flat sides of the bean between your thumb and index finger and slice the edge of the pod between your fingers with a sharp knife. Scrape the marrow out of the pod halves into the egg-sugar mixture. There is a bonus for you here: Put the pod that remains in a canister of sugar and in a week or so your sugar will have a wonderful vanilla fragrance. The sugar is excellent for cakes and cookies.

KWEE PILOW
Doughnuts

About 1-1/4 cups (300 ml) water
4 tablespoons (60 ml) butter
1 cup (250 ml) all-purpose flour
6 egg yolks
Vegetable oil for deep-frying
Super-fine sugar

Combine the water and butter in a saucepan and bring to a boil. Remove from the heat and let cool to lukewarm. With a whisk, beat the flour through the water-butter mixture until it is very smooth. Return the pan to medium heat and cook, stirring constantly, until thick and shiny. Beat the egg yolks until they are very light in color and stir them through the dough in the saucepan. When cool enough to handle, form 1-inch (3 cm) balls of the dough with your hands. Heat the oil in a wok or deep saucepan to a depth of about 1-1/2 inches (4 cm) until very hot (375°F or 190°C). Deep-fry the balls, a few at a time, until golden. Remove with a slotted utensil and drain on paper toweling. Serve warm with sugar sprinkled over them.

THAILAND

The Thai Meal

Thailand, with its tropical climate, monsoon rains, bountiful rivers and seaside proximity, produces a tremendous array of foodstuffs. The people demand a light, spicy cuisine that will stimulate but not overburden the appetite in this hot climate.

Traditionally, the Thai meal is served on the floor on mats or on a low table surrounded by cushions for seating. The table is set with plates and bowls for soup. Most modern Thais eat with a spoon held in the right hand and a fork in the left (if right-handed), though in the past food was held with the fingers. You may want to try this latter technique, as there are many who swear the food tastes better when taken this way. Chopsticks, an adaptation from the Chinese, are frequently used for eating noodle dishes.

All of the dishes of a meal, except dessert, are served at once, and the diner takes from each according to his individual taste. There must always be rice *(cow)* and an average meal would include a curry *(gang pet)* and a soup *(gang chood)*. If one prepares a soupy curry, such as *gang sawm,* or one of the coconut cream-based curries, the soup may be omitted and a vegetable dish substituted. In addition, one could add a salad, such as *lahp,* or an appetizer. One could even cook two types of curries for a meal. The important consideration when selecting the dishes to serve is that there be a balance and a contrast. A spicy curry with a simple stir-fry dish. A crispy texture against a softer one. Salty versus sweet versus sour. An oily dish and a drier one.

For lunch or an afternoon or late-night snack, noodle dishes are popular, though they are not exclusively eaten at these times. Iced tea, beer and *arak* (Thai whiskey) are the beverages mostly commonly served with meals, though hot tea (green or black) may be taken if preferred.

ABOUT THE RECIPES

The recipes that follow make two portions, unless otherwise specified. Thus, two dishes and rice will comprise a meal for two. For gatherings of more than two, increase the number of dishes and the amount of each dish according to the number of people being served. It is not, however, necessary to increase the number of dishes for each additional diner to the extent that the Chinese do. For example, select three recipes, double their amounts and you will be able to serve four generously.

The majority of recipes included here are national favorites and principally from the central region, of which Bangkok is the center. The appearance of a dish is important to the Thais, as is evident in their custom of sculpturing fruit and creating elaborate garnishes—so you should take a bit of time to dress a dish with sprigs of coriander or mint or a similar form of attention. The amount of seasoning and degree of hotness are moderate in these recipes. The reader is encouraged to start with the amounts given and then gradually increase the seasoning to suit individual taste. Those who are not accustomed to hot foods can easily develop a taste for Thai food if they eat small amounts of the spicy items with scoops of rice (and maybe wash it all down with a big swallow of beer). Hot foods go a long way with rice, so don't be shy when it comes to eating it. In fact, the literal translation for "dining" in Thai is "to eat rice."

Rice & Noodles

BOBPEEUH
Egg Rolls

3 ounces (90 g) boned chicken meat, finely minced
3 ounces (90 g) pork shoulder or rump, finely
  minced
2 tablespoons (30 ml) finely minced onion
3 medium dried mushrooms, soaked in warm
  water 15 minutes, drained and finely shredded
1 ounce (30 g) bean-thread noodles, soaked in
  warm water 15 minutes, drained and cut into
  2-inch (5 cm) lengths
1/2 egg, beaten
Egg roll wrappers*
2 teaspoons (10 ml) flour, mixed with
  4 teaspoons (20 ml) water for sealing wrappers
Peanut oil for deep-frying
Chinese plum sauce or Thai sweet chili sauce
  and fish sauce (nam bla)

Combine the chicken, pork, onion, mushrooms, noodles and egg and mix well. Place one of the wrappers on a flat surface. (See page 153.) If it is a square or rectangle, place it with one of the corners nearest you. If it is a quarter of a large circle place it with the round part of the quarter circle nearest you. Put about one eighth of the filling on the third of the wrapper nearest you, a short distance in from the edge. Fold the near edge of the wrapper over the filling, then fold in the sides. With a pastry brush or your fingertips, paint the upper edges of the wrapper with the flour-water paste, then roll up and seal. Repeat until all of the filling is used.

Heat the oil to a depth of 2 inches (5 cm) in a wok or pan and deep-fry the egg rolls 3 minutes, or until golden and crispy. Serve with Chinese plum sauce or Thai sweet chili sauce and fish sauce for dipping. Makes 8 3- to 4-inch (8 to 10 cm) rolls.

*Thai egg roll wrappers, available dried, are made from rice flour and are very large. To use, immerse them in hot water until they become very pliable, then cut into quarters. Though made from wheat flour, imported or domestic Philippine lumpia wrappers, available frozen, can also be used. You may also use commercial fresh or frozen Chinese egg roll or spring roll wrappers (the latter are thinner and therefore preferred). The number of egg rolls you are able to make with this recipe will vary with the size of the skins you use.

MEE KROB
Crisp Fried Noodles

A crispy noodle dish with a sweet sauce.

Peanut oil for deep-frying
4 ounces (125 g) rice vermicelli
1/4 cup (60 ml) water
2 tablespoons (30 ml) tamarind liquid *(som ma kham)* or fresh lime juice
1 tablespoon (15 ml) peanut oil
1 tablespoon (15 ml) chopped red onion
1 garlic clove, crushed
2 ounces (60 g) ground pork
4 medium shrimp, shelled, deveined and coarsely chopped
1 tablespoon (15 ml) tomato paste
2 teaspoons (10 ml) fish sauce *(nam bla)*
1/4 teaspoon (1 ml) monosodium glutamate (optional)
1/2 cup (125 ml) bean sprouts, green "tails" removed (optional)
1 tablespoon (15 ml) chopped fresh coriander
1 tablespoon (15 ml) chopped green onion
1 teaspoon (5 ml) sliced pickled ginger

To deep-fry the rice vermicelli, heat oil to a depth of 2 inches until hot (about 375°F or 190°C). Test the oil temperature by dropping in a few strands of the vermicelli. If they puff and turn golden immediately, the oil is ready. Drop only a small handful of the noodles into the oil at a time. When the noodles puff (they will expand to many times their original size), turn and *very briefly* fry the other side. The entire cooking process should take only a few seconds. Remove with a slotted utensil and drain on paper toweling.

Combine the water, tamarind and sugar in a small saucepan and place over medium-high heat, stirring to dissolve sugar. Boil gently, stirring occasionally, about 5 minutes, or until a syrup is formed. While the syrup is cooking, heat 1 tablespoon (15 ml) peanut oil in a wok, add the red onion and garlic and stir-fry 10 seconds. Add the pork and shrimp and stir-fry 1 minute. Then add the syrup, tomato paste, fish sauce and monosodium glutamate, cover and cook over medium heat 3 minutes. Mix the bean sprouts into the sauce, then thoroughly but *gently* mix the sauce with the noodles. Do not mix hard or the noodles will deflate. Serve on a platter garnished with coriander, green onion and pickled ginger.

COW PAHT
Fried Rice

Thai-style fried rice can be made with meats, poultry or seafood. Even cooked leftovers can be used. It is important that the cooked rice be completely cool before adding to the pan or it will become mushy.

2 tablespoons (30 ml) peanut oil
2 garlic cloves, crushed
2 fresh green chili peppers, coarsely shredded
4 ounces (125 g) pork shoulder, rump or tenderloin, cut in pieces 4 by 1-1/2 by 1/4 inch (10 cm by 4 cm by 6 mm)

3 cups (750 ml) cold cooked long-grain white rice
2 tablespoons (30 ml) fish sauce *(nam bla)*
1 small ripe tomato, diced
2 tablespoons (30 ml) water or chicken stock
1/2 teaspoon (2 ml) monosodium glutamate
  (optional)
1 egg, beaten
1 tablespoon (15 ml) chopped fresh coriander
1 tablespoon (15 ml) chopped green onion

Heat the oil in a wok or skillet, add the garlic, chili peppers and pork and stir-fry 3 minutes over moderate heat, or until pork is tender. Add rice, fish sauce, tomato, water and monosodium glutamate, stir well, cover and cook 1 minute. Briskly stir in the egg, add the coriander and onion, stir and serve.

PAHT THAI
Fried Noodles

This is Thai-style *chow mein*, the national noodle dish. Serve it on a large platter surrounded with dishes of condiments for each diner to season his own portion.

2 tablespoons (30 ml) raw peanuts
2 tablespoons (30 ml) peanut oil
2 garlic cloves, crushed
3 ounces (90 g) pork shoulder or rump, cut into
  matchstick strips
6 ounces (200 g) 1/4-inch-wide (6 mm) flat rice
  noodles, soaked in warm water 15 minutes and drained, or
  8 ounces (250 g) fresh rice noodles
1 tablespoon (15 ml) dried shrimp, soaked in warm
  water 10 minutes and drained
1 teaspoon (5 ml) chopped preserved radish or
  other pickled or salted vegetable
2 ounces (60 g) firm fresh bean curd cakes, cut
  into 1/2-inch (1.5 cm) cubes
2 teaspoons (10 ml) fish sauce *(nam bla)*
1 teaspoon (5 ml) sugar
1/4 teaspoon (1 ml) Asian chili powder
1 teaspoon (5 ml) rice vinegar
2 Chinese leeks or green onions, cut into 1-inch
  lengths (3 cm)
1 egg, beaten (optional)
2 tablespoons (30 ml) water, if needed
Condiments: 1 cup (250 ml) bean sprouts, "tails"
  removed; brown sugar; fish sauce *(nam bla);*
  shredded fresh red or green chili pepper; Asian
  chili powder; lime wedges

Toast the peanuts in a 325°F (160°C) oven for about 10 minutes, or until light brown. Grind them in a mortar or nut grinder and set aside. Heat the oil in a wok or skillet, add the garlic and pork and stir-fry 1 minute. Add the noodles, stir well, then add the ground peanuts, shrimp, radish, bean curd, fish sauce, sugar, chili powder and rice vinegar. Stir-fry for 1-1/2 minutes over medium heat, being careful not to break up noodles. Add leeks or green onions and the egg and stir-fry 1 minute. If noodles are still very firm, add 2 tablespoons water (30 ml), cover and cook 1 minute. Serve with condiments.

Vegetables & Salads

PAHT PAHK I
Stir-fried Vegetables I

Because this dish often accompanies spicy curries, its seasoning is usually rather mild. If you prefer a hotter taste, use the chili pepper in place of the black pepper. You can also vary the vegetables used. Snow peas, water chestnuts, fresh mushrooms and canned miniature corn cobs in any combination are good choices.

1 tablespoon (15 ml) peanut oil
1 garlic clove, crushed
3/4 cup (175 ml) coarsely shredded or sliced
   bamboo shoots
3/4 cup (175 ml) coarsely shredded or sliced celery
2 tablespoons (30 ml) fish sauce (nam bla)
1/2 teaspoon (2 ml) monosodium glutamate
   (optional)
1/4 teaspoon (1 ml) sugar
1/4 teaspoon (1 ml) ground black pepper, or
   1 fresh green chili pepper, coarsely shredded

Heat the oil in a wok or skillet, add the garlic and stir-fry until pungent. Add the bamboo shoots and celery and stir-fry 1 minute. Add all remaining ingredients, stir well, cover and cook until steam rises to surface, about 2 minutes. When done, the vegetables should be tender, yet crisp.

PAHT PAHK II
Stir-fried Vegetables II

1/2 cup (125 ml) Thai or Chinese canned straw
   mushrooms, well drained, or dried Japanese
   shiitake mushrooms, soaked in water to soften
   and tough stems removed
1/2 cup (125 ml) canned miniature corn cobs,
   rinsed
1/2 cup (125 ml) coarsely shredded Chinese
   cabbage (bok choy)*
1 tablespoon (15 ml) peanut oil
1 garlic clove, crushed
1 slice ginger root, crushed with flat side of cleaver
   and peeled
1/4 cup (60 ml) chicken stock
1/2 teaspoon (2 ml) arrowroot, or
   1/4 teaspoon (1 ml) cornstarch
1 teaspoon (5 ml) fish sauce (nam bla)
1/2 teaspoon (3 ml) dark soy sauce

Slice the mushrooms and set aside with the corn cobs and cabbage. Heat the oil in a wok or skillet, add the garlic, ginger and reserved vegetables and stir-fry 1 minute. Add the chicken stock, cover and bring to boil. Dissolve arrowroot in fish sauce and soy sauce and add to wok. Cook and stir just until juices thicken.

*If possible, buy very young bok choy, called choy sum by the Chinese. It is very tender and has small yellow flowers.

PAHT PAHK NAHM MAHN HOI
Greens with Oyster Sauce

Nahm mahn hoi is the Thai name for oyster sauce, a dark-brown, rich extractive of dried oysters that is devoid of fishiness. The finest-flavored oyster sauce is imported from Hong Kong.

1 tablespoon (15 ml) peanut oil
1 large garlic clove, crushed
1 teaspoon (5 ml) Chinese brown bean sauce *(mien see),* mashed, or
    Thai soybean condiment *(dow jeeoh dam)*
8 ounces (250 g) collard greens, sliced across the grain into 2- to 3-inch-wide (5 to 8 cm) pieces
1 tablespoon (15 ml) water
2 tablespoons (30 ml) oyster sauce *(nahm mahn hoi)*
1/4 teaspoon (1 ml) sugar
1/2 teaspoon (2 ml) monosodium glutamate (optional)
1 teaspoon (5 ml) fish sauce *(nam bla)*

Heat the oil in a wok or skillet, add the garlic and stir-fry until pungent. Add the brown bean sauce, then the greens, and stir-fry 1 minute. Add all remaining ingredients, stir well, cover and cook for 30 to 60 seconds, or until greens are tender.

Variations Substitute spinach or Chinese broccoli for the collard greens.

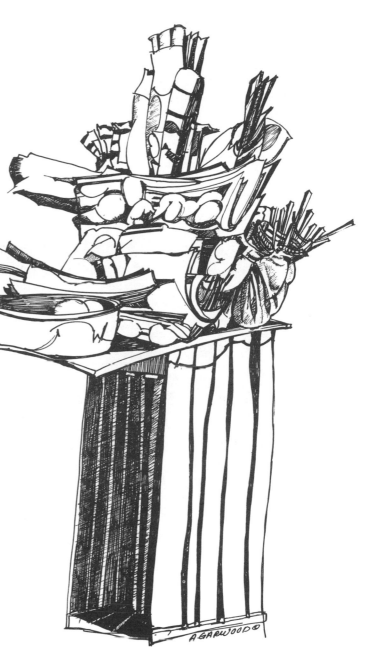

PRIKCHEE SY MOO
Baked Stuffed Chili Peppers

8 ounces (250 g) fresh long mild green chili
   peppers (about 4 inches or 10 cm long)
Peanut oil

Fish stuffing
4 ounces (125 g) fresh white fish fillets, such as
   sole, rock cod, snapper, butterfish or sea bass,
   finely minced
1/2 teaspoon (2 ml) peanut oil
1/2 egg white, lightly beaten
1 teaspoon (5 ml) fish sauce *(nam bla)*
1/4 teaspoon (1 ml) monosodium glutamate
   (optional)
2 water chestnuts, finely minced

Pork stuffing
4 ounces (125 g) pork shoulder or loin, finely
   minced
1 green onion, finely minced
1/4 teaspoon (1 ml) monosodium glutamate
   (optional)
1/2 teaspoon (2 ml) soy sauce

Prepare one of the fillings by combining the ingredients and mixing well. Slice the tops off the chili peppers, discard the tops and remove and discard the seeds. Divide the filling evenly between the peppers, spooning it in carefully so as not to split them. Arrange the peppers in an oiled baking dish, brush them with oil and bake in a preheated 350°F (180°C) oven for 30 minutes.

Variations Substitute fresh small mild green chili peppers for the long ones. Proceed as directed, but bake only 20 minutes, covering the dish with a lid or aluminum foil all but the last 5 minutes of cooking time. These small chilies make excellent appetizers. Or substitute small green bell peppers for the chili peppers, increasing baking time to 40 minutes.

You may steam the stuffed chilies instead of bake them. Place in a single layer in an oiled bowl, allowing enough room between them for good heat circulation. Brush the peppers with oil and steam over gently boiling water 5 to 10 minutes less than the time specified for baking: 20 to 25 minutes for long chilies, 10 to 15 minutes for small chilies, 30 to 35 minutes for bell peppers.

DOW HOO TAWT NAM JIM
Fried Tofu with Peanut Sauce

A light dish that can be served with salad or as an hors d'oeuvre.

1-1/2 tablespoons (22 ml) raw peanuts
2 cups (125 ml) water
1/4 cup (60 ml) sugar
1 tablespoon (15 ml) rice vinegar
1/4 teaspoon (1 ml) salt
2 teaspoons (10 ml) chopped fresh coriander
1/4 teaspoon (1 ml) Asian chili powder
Peanut oil for deep-frying
8 ounces (250 g) deep-fried bean curd cubes*

To prepare the sauce, toast the peanuts in a pre-heated 325°F (160°C) oven 10 minutes, or until light brown. Grind in a mortar or nut grinder and set aside. Combine the water and sugar in a small saucepan and place over medium heat, stirring to dissolve sugar. Boil until syrupy, then add vinegar, reserved peanuts, salt, coriander and chili powder and simmer 1 minute. Remove from heat and cool to room temperature.

Heat 1-1/2 to 2 inches (4 to 5 cm) of oil in a wok or skillet to 350°F (170°C). Deep-fry the bean curd cubes for 30 seconds, then remove with a slotted utensil and drain on paper toweling. Serve bean curd cubes with sauce on the side.

*Deep-fried bean curd cubes are available in Chinese and Japanese markets. If unavailable in your area, this recipe can be prepared with fresh firm bean curd cakes. Cut the cakes into pieces 1-1/2-inch (4 cm) square and deep-fry in peanut oil heated to 375°F (190°C) about 6 to 8 minutes, or until golden brown. Drain on paper toweling. Omit the second frying.

Variation Substitute 1 heaping tablespoon (20 ml) chunky-style peanut butter for the raw peanuts.

FUK TAWNG SY KY
Pumpkin and Eggs

This light, soft, sweet vegetable omelet is a good accompaniment to spicy dishes.

6-ounce wedge (200 g) pumpkin, with skin removed
2 tablespoons (30 ml) peanut oil
1 garlic clove, crushed
2 eggs, beaten
1/4 teaspoon (1 ml) ground black pepper
1 tablespoon (15 ml) fish sauce *(nam bla)*

Lay inner surface of pumpkin wedge on a cutting board, and with a sharp knife held at a 30-degree angle, slice obliquely against the long axis of the wedge into 1/2-inch-thick (1.5 cm) slices. Heat the oil in a wok or skillet and stir-fry the pumpkin and garlic over medium heat until pumpkin is tender. Combine all remaining ingredients and add to wok. Stir until eggs are just set.

PAHT TOOUH NGAWK GAP DOW HOO
Bean Sprouts with Bean Curd

Peanut oil
8 ounces (250 g) firm fresh bean curd cakes, cut
　　into pieces 1 by 2 by 3/4 inch (3 by 5 by 2 cm)
1 garlic clove, crushed
6 ounces (200 g) bean sprouts*
2 tablespoons (30 ml) fish sauce *(nam bla),* or
　　1/2 teaspoon (3 ml) dark soy sauce
1/4 teaspoon (1 ml) sugar
1/4 teaspoon (1 ml) monosodium glutamate
　　(optional)
1 green onion, cut into 2-inch (5 cm) lengths

Heat oil to a depth of 1 inch (3 cm) in a wok or skillet until very hot. Add the bean curd and cook for 5 minutes, or until golden brown. Pour off almost all the oil (it may be strained and reserved for frying bean curd again), add the garlic and bean sprouts and gently stir-fry for 30 seconds. Add all remaining ingredients, cover and cook 30 seconds. Do not overcook; the bean sprouts should retain their crispness.

*If you have the patience, pinch the green "tails" from the bean sprouts. The taste and texture of the dish are much better if you do.

SAWM TAHM
Sour Salad

This Thai-style coleslaw combines unusual flavors and textures: crunchy papaya, nutlike dried shrimp, sour lime, peanuts and seasonings.

1 tablespoon (15 ml) raw peanuts
1 firm green papaya
1 to 2 ounces (30 to 60 g) green beans
2 teaspoons (10 ml) dried shrimp, coarsely
　　chopped
2 fresh green chili peppers, finely shredded
1 teaspoon (5 ml) sugar
1/2 teaspoon (2 ml) monosodium glutamate
1 teaspoon (5 ml) fish sauce *(nam bla)*
Romaine or red leaf lettuce leaves

Toast the peanuts in a preheated 325°F (160°C) oven 10 minutes or until light brown. Chop coarsely and set aside. Peel and seed the papaya. Shred it by passing it slowly through a coarse grater or by cutting it on a board with a cleaver. Shred the green beans to match the papaya pieces. You should have about 1 cup (250 ml) papaya and 1/2 cup (125 ml) green beans. Combine the papaya, green beans, chopped peanuts, shrimp, chili peppers, sugar, monosodium glutamate and fish sauce and mix well. Chill and serve over lettuce leaves.

Variation If an unripe papaya is not available, substitute 1 cup (250 ml) shredded carrot.

YAM BLA
Fish Salad

Though this salad is more properly Chinese than Thai, it is so good it cannot be excluded.

6 ounces (200 g) firm fresh tuna or sea bass fillets, cut into strips 3/4 by 2 by 1/2 inch (2 by 5 by 1.5 cm)
2 teaspoons (10 ml) rice vinegar
1 teaspoon (5 ml) sugar
1/2 teaspoon (3 ml) Oriental-style sesame oil
1/2 teaspoon (3 ml) soy sauce or fish sauce (nam bla)
1/4 teaspoon (1 ml) five-spice powder
Peanut oil for deep-frying
1 ounce (30 g) bean-thread noodles
1-1/2 tablespoons (22 ml) raw peanuts
1 tablespoon (15 ml) sesame seeds
2 tablespoons (30 ml) shredded pickled ginger
3 young green onions, cut into 2-inch (5 cm) lengths
Juice of 1/2 lime

Combine the fish, vinegar, sugar, sesame oil, soy sauce or fish sauce and five-spice powder and mix well. Chill. To deep-fry the bean-thread noodles, heat oil to a depth of 2 inches (5 cm) until hot (about 375°F or 190°C). Test the oil temperature by dropping in a few strands of the bean-thread noodles. If they puff and turn golden immediately, the oil is ready. Drop only a small handful of the noodles into the oil at a time. When the noodles puff (they will expand to many times their original size), turn and very *briefly* fry the other side. The entire cooking process should take only a few seconds. Remove with a slotted utensil and drain on paper toweling.

Toast the peanuts and sesame seeds in a preheated 325°F (160°C) oven 5 minutes for the sesame seeds and 10 minutes for the peanuts, or until light brown. Chop the peanuts and set the peanuts and sesame seeds aside.

Put the fish on a platter and top with the peanuts, sesame seeds, pickled ginger and green onions. Arrange the noodles on top. Just before serving, sprinkle with lime juice and mix together gently.

YUM YAI
Multiflavored Salad

8-ounce-piece (250 g) beef sirloin or flank steak
1 tablespoon (15 ml) fish sauce (nam bla)
1 fresh green chili pepper, finely shredded
Juice of 1/2 medium lime or lemon
1 egg, hard cooked and sliced
Lettuce, sliced cucumbers, tomato wedges
2 tablespoons (30 ml) chopped fresh coriander

Grill the beef over hot charcoal until medium rare. Cut on the diagonal into slices 1/4 to 1/2 by 4 inches (6 mm to 1.5 cm by 10 cm). Mix the beef slices with the fish sauce, chili pepper and lime. Arrange the beef on a platter with the egg slices, lettuce, cucumber and tomato. Garnish with coriander.

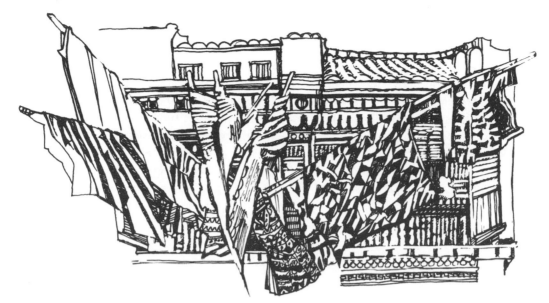

LAHP
Meat Salad

8 ounces (250 g) finest beef tenderloin, sirloin or
   round or tender chicken breast meat
2 teaspoons (10 ml) long-grain white rice
1 tablespoon (15 ml) coarsely chopped fresh
   peppermint leaves
2 teaspoons (10 ml) coarsely chopped fresh
   coriander
1 teaspoon (5 ml) finely shredded red onion
1 teaspoon (5 ml) coarsely chopped green onion
Juice of 1/2 medium lemon or lime
2 teaspoons (10 ml) fish sauce *(nam blu)*
1/4 to 1/2 teaspoon (1 to 2 ml) Asian chili powder
Chilled romaine lettuce leaves

On a cutting board, chop the meat very fine with a
cleaver. (Chopping with a keen edge preserves the
texture and juice, whereas grinding would force
them out, so do not be tempted to put the meat
through a grinder.) Place the meat in a strainer and
immerse in a pot of simmering water for 30 seconds for the beef, 1 minute for the chicken. (It is
important that the chicken be cooked through, so
this step may take even longer than 1 minute.
Leave the chicken in the water until *all* redness has
disappeared.) Remove the meat from the strainer
and drain well; set aside.

Put the rice in a small pan and, shaking the pan
constantly, place over medium heat about 3 minutes, or until the rice is opaque and just beginning
to brown. Put the toasted rice in a mortar or in a
blender container and grind until it is the texture
of fine sand. Combine the ground rice, reserved
meat, peppermint leaves, coriander, red and green
onion, lemon or lime juice, fish sauce and chili
powder and mix well. Taste and adjust seasonings.
Chill and serve with lettuce leaves for each diner to
fill with the meat mixture and eat out of hand.

NAM
Sausage

Nam (rhymes with Sam) is a northern Thai special-ty, the basis of which is a fermented, sour-flavored raw pork sausage eaten fearlessly by the Thais. It is often available in Thai groceries in this country with tongue-in-cheek required advice to cook it. The sweeter-tasting, more coarsely-textured Chinese pork sausage, *lop chiang,* may be substituted in this cooked version.

6 ounces (200 g) Thai or Chinese sausage, cut into
   1/4-inch (6 mm) slices on the diagonal
Juice of 1/2 medium lime
1/2 teaspoon (2 to 3 ml) garlic juice*
2 tablespoons (30 ml) raw peanuts
1 medium red onion, sliced
2 tablespoons (30 ml) thinly sliced pickled ginger
Fresh coriander sprigs
1/2 medium lime, cut into tiny cubes
Chilled romaine lettuce leaves
Asian chili powder
Salt

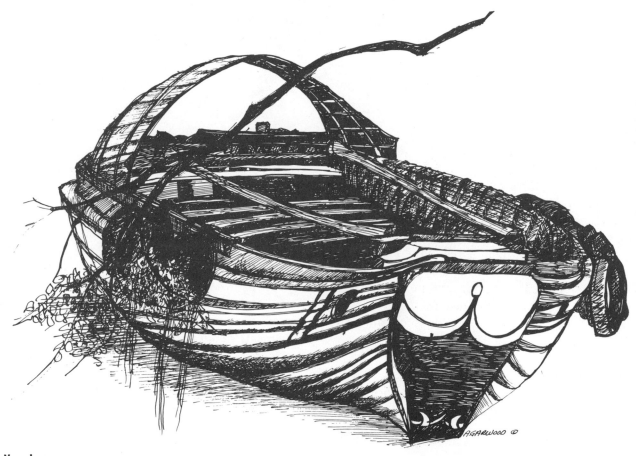

Fry the sausage slices over medium heat until cooked through. (There is no need to add oil to the pan, as the fat in the sausages is released as they cook.) Remove from the pan with a slotted utensil and drain on paper toweling. Sprinkle with lime and garlic juices and chill.

Toast the peanuts in an oven preheated to 325°F (160°C) 10 minutes or until light brown. Coarsely chop the peanuts and arrange them attractively on a large platter with the onion, pickled ginger, coriander sprigs, lime cubes, chilled sausage and lettuce leaves. Place the platter on the dinner table with a container of salt and one of chili powder. Each diner takes a lettuce leaf and piles it with sausage, onion, ginger, coriander, peanuts, lime, chili powder and salt, rolls it up and eats it out of hand.

*You may use garlic juice purchased in a supermarket or prepare your own in the following manner: Crush 1 large garlic clove and put it in a large spoon with 1 teaspoon (5 ml) lime juice. Gently stir to release the garlic essence, then strain for use.

SALAD ACCOMPANIMENTS

Thais often accompany salads with side dishes of pickled vegetables *(pahk dawng)*, cashews or peanuts and shrimp chips (see page 24).

Pickled Cabbage
Slice a small head of Napa cabbage into 1-inch-wide (3 cm) pieces and place in the sun to wilt for a few hours. Transfer the cabbage to a wide-mouth jar and sprinkle with 2 tablespoons (30 ml) of salt. Let stand in a warm place, loosely covered to allow

for ventilation, for 2 to 5 days. The longer it stands, the more fermented it will taste. Put in a jar with a tightly fitting lid and store in the refrigerator.

Pickled Bean Sprouts
Put 4 ounces (125 g) bean sprouts (with tails removed if you have the patience) in a wide-mouth jar. Add 2 teaspoons (10 ml) *each* salt and rice vinegar, 1 teaspoon (5 ml) sugar and 2 tablespoons (30 ml) water saved from washing rice. Now add water to nearly cover sprouts and let stand in a warm place, loosely covered to allow for ventilation, for about 3 days. Put in a jar with a tightly fitting lid and store in the refrigerator. Garlic cloves may be pickled in this same manner.

Deep-fried Cashews
Heat peanut oil in a wok or skillet to 375°F (190°C). Add whole raw cashews and deep-fry until golden brown, about 45 seconds.

Boiled Peanuts
Throughout Thailand, *boiled* peanuts rather than our customary roasted peanuts are a popular snack food. To prepare, simply boil raw peanuts in the shell in lightly salted water for 15 minutes. Drain, cool and serve.

Soups

GWAYTEEO NIUH
Rice Noodle Soup

This easy-to-prepare, light, aromatic beef and noodle soup is a satisfying lunch or late-night snack.

5 cups (1.25 L) water or half water and half home-made or canned beef stock
1 pound (500 g) cracked beef short ribs
2 tablespoons (30 ml) fish sauce *(nam bla)*
1 teaspoon (5 ml) monosodium glutamate (optional)
1/2 teaspoon (2 ml) galangal powder *(ka)*
1 teaspoon (5 ml) ground lemon grass *(da kry)*
4-inch-length (10 cm) celery stalk
4 ounces (125 g) rice vermicelli, soaked in warm water 10 minutes and drained
1-1/2 tablespoons (22 ml) chopped celery leaves
1-1/2 tablespoons (22 ml) chopped fresh coriander
1-1/2 tablespoons (22 ml) chopped green onion
2 tablespoons (30 ml) rice vinegar
1 teaspoon (5 ml) sugar
1 tablespoon (15 ml) tiny vinegar-packed chili peppers *(siling labuyo,* Philippine), or
1/2 teaspoon (2 ml) Asian chili powder
Condiments: rice vinegar, sugar, fish sauce *(nam bla)*, vinegar-packed chili peppers, sliced fresh green chili peppers or Asian chili powder, toasted ground peanuts

Combine the water, short ribs, fish sauce, mono-sodium glutamate, galangal powder, lemon grass and celery stalk in a large saucepan, bring to a boil, lower heat, cover and simmer 40 minutes, or until meat is tender. Remove the short ribs from the stock and cut the meat from the bones; set meat aside. Skim the fat from stock and discard. Heat the stock to boiling, reduce heat slightly and simmer rapidly, uncovered, until stock is reduced to about 3 cups.

Put the rice vermicelli in a colander or strainer and immerse in a large pot of boiling water 1 minute or until tender. Drain well and divide the noodles between 2 large soup bowls. Top each bowl of noodles with half the beef. Evenly divide the celery leaves, coriander, green onions, vinegar, sugar and chili peppers or chili powder between the 2 bowls and pour the boiling stock over the top. Put each of the condiments in a small bowl for each diner to season his soup to his liking.

Variation Half-inch-wide (1.5 cm) fresh rice noodles or 1/4-inch-wide (6 mm) dried rice noodles may be substituted for vermicelli. If using the former, simply bring to room temperature and immerse in boiling water 1 minute as described for rice vermicelli. If using the latter, soak in warm water 20 minutes, drain and immerse in boiling water as described for rice vermicelli, increasing cooking time to 3 minutes.

TAWM YAHM
Multiflavored Soup

This soup is a popular restaurant item—a mildly hot, sour, astringent, aromatic preparation that can be prepared with chicken or shrimp.

6 ounces (200 g) small chicken drumsticks or wings
3 cups chicken stock or water
1/2 to 1 teaspoon (2 to 5 ml) monosodium glutamate (optional)
2 dried citrus leaves *(by maglood)*
2 heaping teaspoons (12 ml) dried lemon grass stalk segments *(da kry)*
Piece of dried galangal root *(ka)* the size of a quarter
2 tablespoons (30 ml) fish sauce *(nam bla)*
4 ounces (125 g) fresh mushrooms, sliced
Juice of 1/2 or 1 medium lime or lemon
1/4 to 1/2 teaspoon (1 to 2 ml) Asian chili powder
1/4 cup (60 ml) coconut cream
1 tablespoon (15 ml) chopped fresh coriander
Thin lime or lemon slices

Bone the chicken and cut the meat into slices about 2 by 4 by 1/4 inch (5 cm by 10 cm by 6 mm); set the meat aside. Combine the chicken bones, chicken stock or water, monosodium glutamate, citrus leaves, lemon grass and fish sauce in a saucepan, bring to a boil, lower heat, cover and simmer 10 minutes. Remove and discard the bones. Add the chicken meat and mushrooms and simmer 2 to 3 minutes, or until chicken is tender. Add the lime juice, chili powder and coconut cream and bring to a boil. Remove from heat and garnish with coriander and lime slices.

Variation Substitute 6 ounces (200 g) medium shrimp, shelled and deveined, for the chicken. Proceed as directed, omitting the chicken bones from the stock or water.

GANG CHOOD WUN SEN
Bean-thread Noodle Soup

Light and bland, this soup, with the interesting texture of bean-thread noodles, is a good accompaniment for spicy dishes.

4 ounces (125 g) pork shoulder, finely minced
White of 1 small egg
3 cups (750 ml) chicken stock
1-1/2 cups (375 ml) coarsely cut Napa cabbage
1 ounce (30 g) bean-thread noodles, soaked in warm water 20 minutes and drained
1 tablespoon (15 ml) fish sauce *(nam bla)*
1/2 teaspoon (2 ml) ground black pepper
2 tablespoons (30 ml) chopped fresh coriander

Mix together the pork and egg white and form into balls 1 inch (3 cm) in diameter. Bring the chicken stock to a boil and add the balls. When the stock returns to the boil, add the cabbage, bean-thread noodles, fish sauce and black pepper. Simmer, uncovered, 3 to 5 minutes, or until balls are cooked. Garnish with coriander.

YENTOFO
Monkey Balls Soup

This hot and sour tomato soup with deep-fried bean curd and fish balls is a meal in itself.

1 quart (1 L) chicken stock
1/2 to 1 pound (250 to 500 g) pork bones
4 ounces (125 g) firm fresh fish fillets, such as sole, halibut, flounder, butterfish or sea bass,* finely cut
1/2 teaspoon (2 ml) regular rice flour
White of 1 small egg
8 ounces (250 g) fresh bean curd cakes, cut into pieces 2 by 1 by 1/2 inch (5 by 3 by 1.5 cm)
Peanut oil for deep-frying
6 ounces (200 g) fresh rice noodles, or 4 ounces (125 g) dried 1/4-inch-wide (6 mm) flat rice noodles, soaked in warm water 20 minutes and drained
1 tablespoon (15 ml) rice vinegar
2 tablespoons (30 ml) tomato paste or canned cured bean curd with chili pepper
1 tablespoon (15 ml) tiny vinegar-packed chili peppers (siling labuyo, Philippine), or 1/2 teaspoon (2 ml) Asian chili powder
1/2 teaspoon (2 ml) monosodium glutamate (optional)
1 tablespoon (15 ml) fish sauce (nam bla)
2 to 6 teaspoons (10 to 30 ml) sugar, or to taste
2 tablespoons (30 ml) chopped fresh coriander
1/2 cup (125 ml) coarsely shredded collard greens or spinach leaves, parboiled

Combine the chicken stock and pork bones, bring to boil, lower heat, cover and simmer at least 20 minutes. While the stock is cooking, pound the fish in a stoneware mortar with a wooden pestle until a thick paste is formed. (You may also use a Chinese cleaver on a cutting board or a blender or food processor for this step.) Mix in the rice flour and egg white and shape into balls 1 inch (3 cm) in diameter. Bring a large pot of water to a boil, drop in the fishballs and cook until they have floated for 1 minute. Lift the fishballs out with a slotted utensil and set aside. Deep-fry the bean curd pieces in the oil 2 minutes, or until golden. Remove with a slotted utensil and drain on paper toweling. Put the fresh or reconstituted dried noodles in a colander and immerse in a large pot of boiling water 1 minute for the fresh noodles and 3 minutes for the dried reconstituted ones, or until tender. Drain well and divide evenly between 2 large bowls. Then divide the vinegar, tomato paste or red bean curd, chili peppers or chili powder, monosodium glutamate, fish sauce, sugar, coriander and collard greens or spinach leaves and fishballs between the bowls. Strain the stock and remove any fat on the surface. Bring the stock to a boil and pour into the bowls. Mix gently and let stand a few minutes for flavors to blend.

*Fresh fish paste is available in Chinese fish markets and is excellent for use in this recipe.

DAWM FANG NAHM
Wintermelon Soup with Spareribs

There are a number of melons popular in Thailand for making soup. *Dawm fang,* or wintermelon, makes a soup that is smooth to the tongue and cool to the taste. The melon ranges in size from 1-1/2 pounds to 20 pounds (750 g to 10 kg) and has light green skin with a slightly powdery look and white to off-white green flesh. These melons, found in Oriental food markets, are sold by the piece as well as whole.

8 ounces (250 g) pork spareribs, cut into 1-1/2-
   inch (4 cm) lengths
3 cups (750 ml) water or chicken stock
2 tablespoons (30 ml) fish sauce *(nam bla)*
1 teaspoon (5 ml) monosodium glutamate
   (optional)
1-1/4-pound-wedge (625 g) wintermelon,
   peeled and cut into 2-inch (5 cm) cubes

Combine the spareribs, water, fish sauce and monosodium glutamate in a saucepan, bring to a boil, lower heat and simmer, covered, 30 minutes, skimming any froth that forms on the surface. Add the wintermelon and simmer until melon flesh is transparent, about 10 minutes.

BAMEE NAHM
Egg Noodle Soup

8 ounces (250 g) fresh egg noodles *(bamee)* *
3 cups (750 ml) chicken stock
1 cup (250 ml) cooked chopped chicken, beef,
   seafood or Chinese roast pork *(moo dang)*
2 tablespoons (30 ml) chopped green onion
2 tablespoons (30 ml) chopped fresh coriander
2 tablespoons (30 ml) chopped celery leaves
1/2 teaspoon (3 ml) Oriental-style sesame oil
Condiments: Asian chili powder, fish sauce *(nam bla),* tiny vinegar-packed chili peppers, sesame oil

Bring a large pot of water to a boil and add the noodles. When the water returns to the boil, add 1 cup (250 ml) cold water. When the water returns to the boil a second time, drain the noodles and divide between 2 large bowls. Bring the chicken stock to a boil. Divide the meat or seafood, onions, coriander, celery leaves and sesame oil evenly between the 2 bowls and pour the boiling stock over the top. Put each of the condiments in a small bowl for each diner to season his soup to his liking.

*These are the same as Chinese *mein,* which are more readily available than Thai noodles and can be substituted. You may also substitute dried noodles for the fresh. Those imported from Taiwan and Hong Kong are suitable. Use only 4 ounces (125 g) of dried and cook as directed in recipe, but bring to the boil three times rather than twice.

Curries

Curries are the most distinctive dishes of Thai cuisine. Meats, poultry, fish, shellfish and vegetables are cooked with various broths, seasonings and a basic curry flavoring, usually in paste form, that is prepared in advance. Curries can be fruity, sour, sweet, salty, bitter, fishy, meaty, pungent, astringent, or various combinations of these flavors. This cacaphony of flavors is matched as well by regional and ethnic variations in recipes.

In Thailand, one usually purchases a few ounces of a particular curry mixture at shops, where they are made up fresh daily. The most popular curry mixtures are now imported to this country and can be purchased at groceries specializing in Thai foods. They come powdered in small plastic packets and in cans, and should be freshened with a few teaspoons (15 to 20 ml) of water per ounce (30 g) of powder before using.

Once you have experienced the extraordinary flavors of Thai curries, you may not be content with the prepackaged mixtures and will want to prepare them from scratch from one of the following recipes of some of the most popular curry pastes. Preparing your own is not that difficult as the mixtures are actually permutations of fewer ingredients than one might expect. A shelf laden with a dozen jars and packages can be the basis for a hundred different dishes.

In the following curry recipes, "1 package" of curry mixture refers to the 3/4-ounce (21 g) size. This amount results in a mild to moderately spicy dish. Many Thais would double or triple this amount. This intensifying of the seasoning is done with a balancing of the flavors in mind: hot and sweet, salty and sweet, very sour with very hot, and so on. After some experimentation, you can adjust the amount of curry paste to your taste.

Some of the curries that rely on coconut cream for their richness and sweetness may be prepared with chicken stock replacing some or all of the coconut cream. If it is impossible to obtain coconut cream or fresh coconut, one may use an *ersatz* extract made by warming equal amounts of light cream with unsweetened dried grated coconut, then straining the liquid for use.

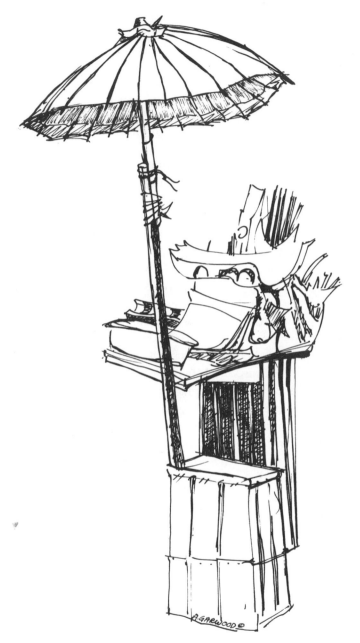

FRESH CURRY PASTES

The traditional Thai method of preparing a curry paste demands 15 minutes of pulverizing all the ingredients together in a stoneware mortar with a wooden pestle. To give the curry paste more body, especially if coconut cream is absent from the recipe, uncooked rice is soaked in a little water for 30 minutes to 1 hour, then pounded along with the other items.

An equally acceptable method of making the paste is to combine all the ingredients with a little water in the small-jar attachment of a blender and blend at high speed until well mixed. The paste should then stand for 30 minutes to "ripen" before using. The fresh herbs and spices used in Thailand are difficult to find here, so I have specified their dry equivalent in the following recipes.

Gang Pet

2 to 4 dried *jalapeño* chili peppers, or
   1 dried cayenne pepper, coarsely chopped
1/2 teaspoon (2 ml) ground lemon grass *(da kry)*
1/2 teaspoon (2 ml) galangal powder *(ka),* or
   1/4 teaspoon (1 ml) ground ginger
2 garlic cloves
1/2 teaspoon (2 ml) dried shrimp paste *(gapee)*
1/2 teaspoon (2 ml) dried citrus peel *(pew maglood),* or
   1 teaspoon (5 ml) grated fresh lemon rind
2 teaspoons (10 ml) minced red onion
1 teaspoon (5 ml) cooked long-grain white rice

Gang Ba

2 to 4 dried *jalapeño* chili peppers, or
   1 dried cayenne pepper, coarsely chopped
1 teaspoon (5 ml) minced red onion
1 garlic clove
1/4 teaspoon (1 ml) galangal powder *(ka)*, or
   1/8 teaspoon (0.5 ml) ground ginger
1/2 teaspoon (3 ml) dried citrus peel *(pew maglood)*, or
   1 teaspoon (5 ml) grated fresh lemon rind
1/4 teaspoon (1 ml) ground lemon grass *(da kry)*
1 teaspoon (5 ml) ground aromatic ginger *(kachai)*

Gang Karee

2 to 4 dried *jalapeño* chili peppers, or
   1 dried cayenne pepper, coarsely chopped
1 garlic clove
1 teaspoon (5 ml) minced red onion
1/2 teaspoon (2 ml) ground coriander
1/4 teaspoon (1 ml) ground cumin
1/2 teaspoon (3 ml) ground lemon grass *(da kry)*
1/2 teaspoon (3 ml) ground turmeric
1/2 teaspoon (3 ml) peanut oil

Choo Chee

2 to 4 dried *jalapeño* chili peppers, or
   1 dried cayenne pepper, coarsely chopped
2 garlic cloves
1 teaspoon (5 ml) dried shrimp paste *(gapee)*
1/4 teaspoon (1 ml) salt

Mus Sa Mun

2 to 4 dried *jalapeño* chili peppers, or
   1 dried cayenne pepper, coarsely chopped
2 garlic cloves
1 teaspoon (5 ml) ground lemon grass *(da kry)*
1 teaspoon (5 ml) peanut oil
2 teaspoons (10 ml) minced red onion
1 teaspoon (5 ml) sugar
1/4 teaspoon (1 ml) ground cumin
1/4 teaspoon (1 ml) ground cardamom
1/4 teaspoon (1 ml) salt

Gang Sawm

2 to 4 dried *jalapeño* chili peppers, or
   1 dried cayenne pepper, coarsely chopped
1 teaspoon (5 ml) ground lemon grass *(da kry)*
2 teaspoons (10 ml) minced red onion
1/2 teaspoon (3 ml) dried shrimp paste *(gapee)*
3 tablespoons (45 ml) tamarind liquid *(som ma kham)*

Keal Wan

2 to 4 fresh green chili peppers, coarsely chopped
2 garlic cloves
1 teaspoon (5 ml) ground lemon grass *(da kry)*
1/4 teaspoon (1 ml) ground turmeric
1/2 teaspoon (2 ml) salt
1/2 teaspoon (2 ml) dried shrimp paste *(gapee)*

GANG SAWM
Sour Curry

This is a hot-and-sour soupy fish curry.

1-1/2 cups (375 ml) water
2 tablespoons (30 ml) fish sauce *(nam bla)*
One 8-ounce (250 g) whole fresh fish (sole,
    butterfish, sea bass, etc.), cleaned, or
    6 ounces (200 g) fresh fish fillets (choice as
    above)
1 to 2 packages (3/4 ounce or 21 g *each*) or 1 to 2
    recipes *gang sawm* curry paste (page 73)
Juice of 1 medium lemon
1/4 teaspoon (1 ml) sugar
1/4 teaspoon (1 ml) monosodium glutamate
    (optional)
1 cup (250 ml) vegetable combination of choice:
    sliced bamboo shoots, green beans cut into
    2-inch (5 cm) lengths, cabbage cut into 1-inch-
    wide (3 cm) wedges, broccoli flowerets

Bring the water and fish sauce to a boil in a saucepan. Add the fish or fish fillets and simmer gently, uncovered, 7 to 10 minutes, or until fish is cooked. Remove the fish or fish fillets from the cooking liquid and reserve liquid. If using a whole fish, skin and bone it. Put the boned fish or fish fillets in a large stoneware mortar with the cooking liquid and add the lemon juice, curry paste, sugar and monosodium glutamate. Pound with a wooden pestle until the mixture forms a paste. (This step can also be done in a blender, in which case it will take only a few seconds of blending at moderate speed, or in a food processor.) Return the fish mixture to the saucepan and bring just to the boiling point. Add the vegetables and simmer, uncovered, 5 to 10 minutes, or until tender.

GANG BA
Fish Curry

1 package (3/4 ounce or 21 g) or 1 recipe *gang ba*
    curry paste (page 73)
2 teaspoons (10 ml) peanut oil
6 ounces (200 g) fresh fish steaks (halibut, cod
    or salmon), cut into 1-inch (3 cm) cubes
6 ounces (200 g) vegetables of choice:
    green beans cut into 2-inch (5 cm) lengths,
    coarsely sliced green bell peppers or chili
    peppers, peeled eggplant cut into pieces 4 by
    2 by 1/2 inch (10 by 5 by 1.5 cm) and shelled
    green peas, or any combination
2 teaspoons (10 ml) fish sauce *(nam bla)*
1/2 teaspoon (2 ml) sugar
1/4 teaspoon (1 ml) monosodium glutamate
    (optional)
1/4 cup (50 ml) water

Combine the curry paste and oil in a wok or skillet placed over medium heat and fry 1 minute, or until pungent. Add the fish and vegetables and stir-fry 1 minute. Add the fish sauce, sugar, monosodium glutamate and water, stir well, cover and cook 2 minutes.

NAM PRIK NAM YA
Fish Sauce

A sweet fish curry sauce served over noodles.

3/4 cup (200 ml) water
3/4 cup (200 ml) coconut cream
1/2 teaspoon (3 ml) galangal powder *(ka)*
1/2 teaspoon (3 ml) ground aromatic ginger
   (kachai)
1 dried citrus leaf *(by maglood)*
One 8-ounce (250 g) whole fresh fish (sole, sea
   bass, butterfish, etc.), cleaned, or
   6 ounces (200 g) fresh fish fillets (choice
   as above)
1-1/2 tablespoons (22 ml) *nam ya* powder, or
   1/2 ounce (15 g) *nam ya* paste*
2 teaspoons (10 ml) fish sauce *(nam bla)*
1/2 teaspoon (2 ml) sugar
1/4 teaspoon (1 ml) monosodium glutamate
   (optional)
8 ounces (250 g) rice vermicelli, soaked in warm
   water 10 minutes and drained
Fresh coriander sprigs

Bring water, half the coconut cream, galangal powder, ginger and the citrus leaf to a boil in a saucepan. Add the whole fish or fish fillets and simmer gently, uncovered, 7 to 10 minutes, or until fish is cooked. Remove the fish or fish fillets from the cooking liquid and reserve the liquid. If using a whole fish, skin and bone it, finely chop the meat and return the meat to the cooking liquid. If using fillets, finely chop them and return the meat to the cooking liquid.

While the fish is cooking, combine the *nam ya* and the remaining coconut cream in a small saucepan and place over medium-high heat until pungent, stirring often. Add to the fish and broth along with the fish sauce, sugar and monosodium glutamate. Simmer, uncovered, 10 minutes, or until very thick.

Put the rice vermicelli in a colander or strainer and immerse in a large pot of boiling water for about 1 minute, or until tender. Drain well and arrange on a platter. Cover with the sauce and garnish with coriander sprigs.

*Available in powdered form or canned as a paste.

CHOO CHEE I
Fried Fish with Curry I

One 12-ounce (375 g) kingfish or trout, cleaned
  with head and tail intact
Peanut oil for deep-frying
2 packages (3/4 ounce or 21 g *each*) or double
  recipe *choo chee* curry paste (page 73)
3/4 cup (200 ml) coconut cream
1 tablespoon (15 ml) fish sauce *(nam bla)*
1/4 teaspoon (1 ml) sugar
1/4 teaspoon (1 ml) monosodium glutamate
  (optional)
2 tablespoons (30 ml) water
Fresh coriander sprigs

Heat oil to a depth of 1-1/2 inches (4 cm) in a wok
or large skillet until almost smoking (400°F or
210°C). Put the fish into the oil and fry until the
skin is dark brown. Turn and fry the second side.
This should take about 8 to 10 minutes in all.
Drain the fish on paper toweling.

    While the fish is cooking, combine the curry
paste and coconut cream in a small saucepan and
place over medium-high heat until pungent, stirring
often. Add the fish sauce, sugar, monosodium
glutamate and water and simmer, uncovered, 5
minutes. Place the fish on a platter, cover with the
sauce and garnish with coriander sprigs.

CHOO CHEE II
Fried Fish with Curry II

1 package (3/4 ounce or 21 g) or 1 recipe *choo
  chee* curry paste (page 73)
2 tablespoons (30 ml) peanut oil
8 ounces (250 g) fresh fish fillets or slices (4 by 2
  by 1/2 inch or 10 by 5 by 1.5 cm), such as
  sole, sea bass, rock cod, butterfish or red
  snapper
1 tablespoon (15 ml) fish sauce *(nam bla)*
1/2 teaspoon (2 ml) sugar
1/4 teaspoon (1 ml) monosodium glutamate
  (optional)
1/4 cup (60 ml) matchstick-cut bamboo shoots
  (optional)
1/4 cup (60 ml) matchstick-cut carrots, parboiled
  3 minutes and drained (optional)
1 tablespoon (15 ml) water

Combine the curry paste and oil in a wok placed
over medium heat and fry 1 minute, or until
pungent. Add the fish and stir-fry gently 1 minute.
Add the fish sauce, sugar, monosodium glutamate,
bamboo shoots, carrots and water and stir-fry 2
minutes, or until fish is cooked.

GANG KEAL WAN GOONG
Green Shrimp Curry

2 packages (3/4 ounce or 21 g *each*) or double
   recipe *keal wan* curry paste (page 73)
1/2 cup (125 ml) coconut cream
2 small fresh green chili peppers, coarsely shredded
   (optional)
6 ounces (200 g) shrimp, shelled and deveined
2 dried citrus leaves *(by maglood)*
3/4 cup (200 ml) shelled green peas, parboiled 5
   minutes and drained

2 tablespoons (30 ml) water
2 teaspoons (10 ml) fish sauce *(nam bla)*
1 tablespoon (15 ml) chopped fresh basil *(by
   holapa)*

Combine the curry paste, coconut cream and chili
peppers in a saucepan and place over medium-high
heat until pungent, stirring often. Add the shrimp,
citrus leaves and peas and simmer, uncovered, 2
minutes. Add the water and fish sauce, cover and
simmer 2 to 3 minutes, or until shrimp are cooked.
Stir in basil and serve.

GAI TAWM KA
Chicken with Galangal

This soupy, mildly hot chicken curry, enough for four to six persons, is flavored with coconut cream and galangal, an Asian root similar to ginger. The flavor of the dish improves with a few hours of sitting time.

One 3- to 4-pound (1.5 to 2 kg) fryer chicken
1 tablespoon (15 ml) galangal powder *(ka)*
1-1/2 teaspoons (7 ml) ground lemon grass *(da kry)*
Juice of 1 medium lime
3 tablespoons (45 ml) fish sauce *(nam bla)*
1 teaspoon (5 ml) monosodium glutamate
   (optional)
1-1/2 cups (375 ml) coconut cream
3 cups (750 ml) water
2 fresh *serrano* chili peppers, coarsely shredded*
2 tablespoons (30 ml) chopped fresh coriander

Cut the chicken into pieces on the bone about 1-1/2 inches (4 cm) square. Combine the chicken, galangal powder, lemon grass, lime juice, fish sauce, monosodium glutamate, coconut cream, water and chili peppers in a heavy saucepan. Bring quickly to a boil, then lower heat and simmer briskly uncovered for 15 minutes or until chicken is tender. Stir often during cooking period. Mix in the coriander and serve.

*The tiny vinegar-packed chilies called *siling labuyo* (Philippine) are also very good in this dish. They are about 3/4 inch (2 cm) long and are sold in jars. Use 2 tablespoons (30 ml) of these chilies in place of the *serrano* chili peppers called for in the recipe.

GANG PET GAI
Chicken Curry

1 package (3/4 ounce or 21 g) or 1 recipe *gang pet* curry paste (page 72)
3/4 cup (200 ml) coconut cream
2 small fresh green chili peppers, coarsely shredded
1/2 cup (125 ml) sliced bamboo shoots
6 ounces (200 g) boned chicken meat, cut into slices 4 by 2 by 1/2 inch (10 by 5 by 1.5 cm), or 12 ounces (375 g) chicken on the bone, cut into 1-inch (3 cm) squares
2 teaspoons (10 ml) fish sauce *(nam bla)*
2 tablespoons (30 ml) water
1/2 teaspoon (2 ml) sugar
1/2 teaspoon (2 ml) monosodium glutamate
   (optional)
2 tablespoons (30 ml) chopped fresh mint

Combine the curry paste and coconut cream in a saucepan and place over medium-high heat until pungent, stirring often. Add the chili pepper, bamboo shoots and chicken and simmer 1 minute. Add the fish sauce, water, sugar and monosodium glutamate and simmer, covered, about 4 minutes, or until chicken is cooked. Remove from the heat, add the mint, stir well, cover and let stand 1 minute before serving.

GANG KAREE
Indian-style Chicken Curry

Karee is the Thai transliteration of the Indian word for curry, while *gang* is the true Thai word for curry. This recipe is called *gang karee* because it contains turmeric (which gives it its beautiful yellow color), coriander and cumin, ingredients commonly found in Indian curries.

1 package (3/4 ounce or 21 g) or 1 recipe *gang karee* paste (page 73)
2 tablespoons (30 ml) peanut oil, or
    1/4 cup (60 ml) coconut cream
1 medium chicken breast, cut into 1-1/2-inch
    (4 cm) pieces on the bone, or
    10 ounces (300 g) chicken legs or wings, cut into
    1-1/2-inch (4 cm) pieces on the bone
1 teaspoon (5 ml) fish sauce *(nam bla)*
2 to 4 tablespoons (30 to 60 ml) water

Combine the curry paste and oil or coconut cream in a wok placed over medium heat and cook, stirring, 1 minute, or until pungent. Add the chicken and stir-fry 2 minutes. Add the fish sauce and water, stir well, cover and simmer 3 minutes, or until chicken is cooked.

PAHT PRIK KING
Peppery Curry with Pork

This is a salty pork and string bean curry with a dry, clinging sauce. It is a quick dish to prepare that is truly outstanding when the proper ingredients are used. The Thais use side pork, which is uncured, unsalted bacon. The pork can be purchased at Oriental butcher shops or special ordered from your butcher. Cooked properly, the side pork releases much of its fat and becomes incredibly tender. Pork shoulder or butt may be substituted, but it must be tender and cooked for less time than specified in the recipe so that it does not toughen. Young green beans, either foot-long (30 cm) Chinese ones or Kentucky Wonders, add a sweetness to the dish that complements the salty *prik king* curry mixture (available at Thai groceries) and the delicately fishy *nam bla*.

1 package (3/4 ounce or 21 g) *prik king* curry
    mixture
1 tablespoon (15 ml) peanut oil
6 ounces (200 g) side pork, cut into 1/4-inch-thick
    (6 mm) slices
6 ounces (200 g) green beans, cut into 1-1/2-inch
    (4 cm) lengths
1 tablespoon (15 ml) fish sauce *(nam bla)*
1/2 teaspoon (2 ml) sugar
1/4 teaspoon (1 ml) monosodium glutamate
    (optional)
2 to 3 tablespoons (30 to 45 ml) water

Combine the curry mixture and oil in a wok placed over medium heat and fry 1 minute, or until pungent. Add the pork and stir-fry gently 10 minutes, or until pork is cooked. Turn up heat to high and add the green beans, fish sauce, sugar, monosodium glutamate and water. Stir-fry 2 minutes, then lower heat to medium, cover and cook 1 minute. Do not overcook the beans; they should be tender yet crisp.

NAM PRIK ONG
Northern-style Curry Sauce

Serve this sweet, tomatoey ground pork curry sauce over steamed rice or boiled or pan-fried flat rice noodles. Accompany with chilled raw, matchstick-cut vegetables, such as cucumbers, carrots or green beans.

1 package (3/4 ounce or 21 g) or 1 recipe *gang pet* curry paste (page 72)
2 teaspoons (10 ml) peanut oil
8 ounces (250 g) ground pork
1 large ripe tomato, chopped
1 tablespoon (15 ml) fish sauce *(narn bla)*
1/2 teaspoon (2 ml) monosodium glutamate (optional)
1/2 to 1-1/2 teaspoons (2 to 7 ml) sugar

Combine the curry mixture and oil in a wok placed over medium heat and fry 1 minute, or until pungent. Add the pork and stir-fry 1 minute, breaking up all the lumps. Add the tomato, fish sauce, monosodium glutamate and sugar and simmer uncovered, 10 minutes, or until mixture becomes very thick.

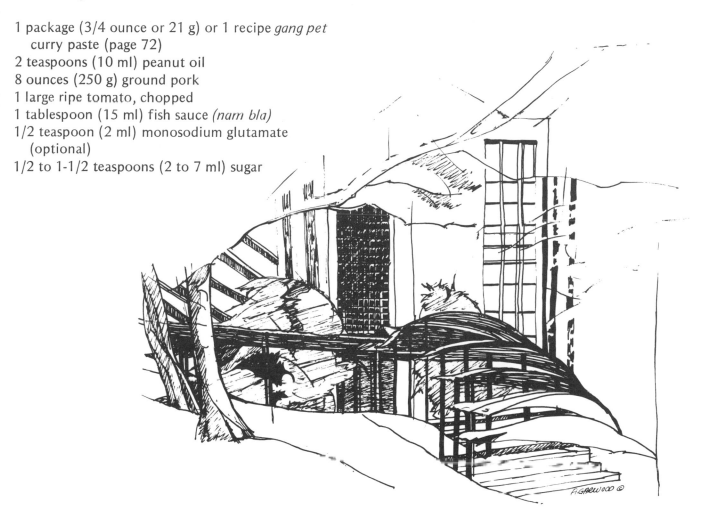

GANG MUS SA MUN
Beef Curry with Potatoes and Peanuts

This sweet and mildly spiced beef stew is a favorite of Westerners in Thailand.

10 ounces (300 g) beef chuck or bottom round, cut into 1-1/2-inch (4 cm) cubes
1 cup (250 ml) water
1 cup (250 ml) coconut cream
1 tablespoon (15 ml) fish sauce *(nam bla)*
1 package (3/4 ounce or 21 g) or 1 recipe *mus sa mun* curry paste (page 73)
Juice of 1 medium lime
1 large potato, peeled and cut into 1-1/2-inch (4 cm) cubes
1 small onion, cut into wedges
3 tablespoons (45 ml) raw peanuts
1 teaspoon (5 ml) sugar, or more to taste
1/2 teaspoon (2 ml) monosodium glutamate (optional)

Combine the beef, water, half the coconut cream and the fish sauce in a saucepan and simmer, uncovered, 20 minutes or until meat is almost tender. While the beef is cooking, combine the curry paste and the remaining 1/2 cup (125 ml) coconut cream in a saucepan and place over medium-high heat until pungent, stirring often. Add the beef and its cooking liquid, lime juice, potato, onion, peanuts, sugar and monosodium glutamate to the curry mixture and simmer slowly, uncovered, until the potato and onion are tender.

GANG KEAL WAN NOOUH
Green Beef Curry

2 packages (3/4 ounce or 21 g *each*) or double recipe *keal wan* curry paste (page 73)
3 ounces (90 ml) coconut cream
2 small fresh green chili peppers, coarsely shredded (optional)
6 ounces (200 g) tender cut of beef, chopped or sliced
2 dried citrus leaves *(by maglood)*
6 ounces (200 g) young spinach leaves, trimmed
2 teaspoons (10 ml) fish sauce *(nam bla)*
2 tablespoons (30 ml) water
1 tablespoon (15 ml) chopped fresh basil *(by holapa)*

Combine the curry paste, coconut cream and chili peppers in a saucepan and place over medium-high heat until pungent, stirring often. Add the beef and citrus leaves and simmer, uncovered, a few minutes. Add the spinach, fish sauce and water and simmer until spinach is tender. Stir in basil and serve.

Seafood

TAWT MON BLA
Fried Fishcakes

These deep-fried curried fishcakes are an excellent appetizer.

6 ounces (200 g) firm fresh fish fillets, such as
   sole, halibut, flounder, butterfish or sea bass*
1 tablespoon (15 ml) *gang pet* curry paste (page 72)
1 teaspoon (5 ml) fish sauce *(nam bla)*
1 egg white
2 ounces (60 g) green beans, finely shredded
1/4 teaspoon (2 ml) cornstarch
Peanut oil for deep-frying

Dipping sauce
1 tablespoon (15 ml) raw peanuts
1/4 teaspoon (1 ml) salt
Juice of 1/2 lime
1 tablespoon (15 ml) water
1/8 teaspoon (0.5 ml) Asian chili powder
2 teaspoons (10 ml) sugar
1/2 teaspoon (3 ml) chopped fresh coriander
1 medium cucumber, thinly sliced

To prepare the dipping sauce, combine all ingredients and mix well. Set aside while making the fishcakes.

Pound the fish fillets, curry paste and fish sauce in a mortar until a thick paste is formed. (You may also use a Chinese cleaver on a cutting board or a blender or food processor for this step.) Mix in the egg white, green beans and cornstarch and form mixture into slightly flattened cakes about 3 inches (8 cm) in diameter.

Heat the oil in a wok or skillet to a depth of about 2 inches (5 cm) until hot (about 375°F or 190°C). Deep-fry the fishcakes, a couple at a time, about 3 minutes, or until golden brown and crispy. Remove with a slotted utensil and drain on paper toweling. Serve with the dipping sauce.

*Fresh fish paste is available in Chinese fish markets and is excellent for use in this recipe.

PAHT BY KAPROW
Squid Fried with Mint

Meat, poultry or seafood stir-fried with mint is a popular Thai dish. It is especially delicious when prepared with squid or chicken.

6 to 8 ounces (200 to 250 g) small squid
1 tablespoon (15 ml) peanut oil
2 to 4 fresh green chili peppers, coarsely shredded
1 large garlic clove, crushed
1/4 cup (60 ml) coarsely chopped fresh mint *(by kaprow)*, or
   2 tablespoons (30 ml) crumbled dried mint
2 tablespoons (30 ml) fish sauce *(nam bla)*
1/2 teaspoon (3 ml) dark soy sauce (optional)
1/2 teaspoon (2 ml) monosodium glutamate (optional)
1/4 teaspoon (1 ml) sugar

Rinse the squid in cold water. Separate the tentacles from the tail section by gently pulling apart, being careful not to break the ink sac. Discard the ink sac and the transparent, sword-shaped cartilege in the tail section. Cut off the tentacles above the eye section and discard the eye section. Force out the small round cartilege at the base of the tentacles with your fingertips, discard the cartilege, and set the tentacles aside. Rinse the tail section and pull off the blotchy membrane. Slice the tail section open lengthwise, then cut into 1-1/2-inch (4 cm) squares. Make shallow Xs on the squares with the point of a knife to ensure tenderness. Set squid aside.

   Heat the oil in a wok or skillet, add the chili peppers and garlic and stir-fry until pungent. Add the mint and squid and stir-fry 1 minute. Add all remaining ingredients, stir well, cover and cook for 30 to 60 seconds or until squid is done. Be careful not to overcook the squid or it will toughen.

HO MOK
Steamed Fish Custard

1/2 cup (125 ml) grated fresh coconut meat
6 ounces (200 g) fresh white fish fillets (sole, rock cod, snapper, butterfish or sea bass) or shrimp meat, *finely* minced (about 1 cup or 250 ml)
2 Chinese leeks, finely minced, or
   1 green onion, finely minced
1/2 cup (125 ml) coconut cream
1 small egg, beaten
1/4 teaspoon (1 ml) sugar
1 to 2 teaspoons (5 to 10 ml) *gang pet* curry paste (page 72), or to taste
Large pieces of banana leaf (optional)

Combine the coconut meat, fish, leeks or green onion, coconut cream, egg, sugar and curry paste and mix well. If using banana leaves, scald them or hold them over the heat to make them pliable. Mound some of the fish mixture in the center of each banana leaf and fold in the sides to make a secure bundle. Fasten closed with bamboo skewers, wooden picks or heavy thread. Alternately, divide the mixture into 4 to 6 glass custard cups (1/2 cup or 125 ml size). Steam over gently boiling water about 15 minutes if in custard cups, 20 minutes if in banana leaves.

Variations Substitute minced chicken meat or pork for the fish. Increase cooking time 5 minutes.

BOO PAHT TAWN GA TIEM
Crab with Leeks

1 live Dungeness crab*
1 tablespoon (15 ml) peanut oil
2 garlic cloves, crushed
2 teaspoons (10 ml) Chinese brown bean sauce
  (mien see), mashed, or
  Thai soybean condiment *(dow jeeoh dam)*
Chinese leeks cut into 2-inch (5 cm) lengths to
  make 1/2 cup (125 ml)**
2 teaspoons (10 ml) fish sauce *(nam bla)*
2 tablespoons (30 ml) water
1/2 teaspoon (2 ml) monosodium glutamate
  (optional)
1/2 teaspoon (2 ml) sugar

To kill the crab, lay it on its back on a firm surface, such as a cutting board, and place a Chinese cleaver, blade edge down, on the center of the crab body. With a mallet, firmly strike the top of the knife blade. Wash the crab under cold running water and pull or twist off the legs and claws. Then pull off the top (back) shell, using a knife to pry it loose if necessary. Carefully remove the crab "butter" for use in the recipe, if desired, or reserve for another use. Remove and discard the innards. Cut the body in half lengthwise, then in quarters. Crack and disjoint the claws and legs with a heavy knife or mallet. Set the crab aside.

Heat the oil in a wok or skillet, add the garlic and bean sauce and stir-fry until pungent. Add the crab and stir-fry 2 minutes. Add all remaining ingredients, cover and cook 4 to 5 minutes, or until crab is done.

*If a live crab is not available, you may use a fresh cooked one. Clean and crack the crab as directed, but stir-fry only 1 minute and cook covered only 3 minutes.

**Chinese leeks are very delicate in flavor. If unavailable, substitute Western chives in the same amount, but increase the garlic to 2 cloves, or substitute very young, tender Western leeks.

HOI PAHT BY HOLAPA
Clams Fried with Basil

A quick, light dish that is good as a first course, as it whets the appetite.

1 pound (500 g) small clams in the shell, such as
  steamers or butter clams
2 tablespoons (30 ml) peanut oil
2 to 4 fresh green chili peppers, coarsely shredded
2 garlic cloves, crushed
1/4 cup (60 ml) coarsely chopped fresh basil *(by
  holapa),* or
  2 tablespoons crumbled dried basil
1 tablespoon (15 ml) fish sauce *(nam bla)*
1/2 teaspoon (3 ml) dark soy sauce
1/2 teaspoon (2 ml) monosodium glutamate
  (optional)

Scrub the clams well and place in cold water to cover for 20 minutes. Drain and set aside. Heat the oil in a wok or skillet, add the chili peppers and garlic and stir-fry until pungent. Add the clams and stir-fry for 30 seconds. Add all remaining ingredients, stir well and cover. In about 30 seconds, the clams will begin to open, releasing their juices and completing the delicious gravy of this dish. When all the clams have opened, remove from heat and serve. (Discard any clams that fail to open.)

NAM PRIK GAPEE
Fermented Shrimp Sauce

A plate of steamed vegetables, served either at room temperature or chilled, crispy fried fish and spicy, pungent *gapee* sauce is a light dish popular with Thais and Burmese.

4 cups (1 L) prepared vegetables of choice:
    green beans cut into 2-inch (5 cm) lengths;
    small cauliflower or broccoli flowerets; sliced
    zucchini or other squash, bamboo shoots or
    carrots; coarsely shredded cabbage
Peanut oil for deep-frying
One 12-ounce (375 g) kingfish, cleaned

Sauce
1 teaspoon (5 ml) dried shrimp paste *(gapee)*
Juice of 1 medium lemon or lime
1 garlic clove, chopped
2 fresh medium green chili peppers, chopped
2 tablespoons (30 ml) chopped tomato
1 teaspoon (5 ml) sugar
1/2 teaspoon (2 ml) monosodium glutamate
    (optional)

To make the sauce, combine all the ingredients in a mortar or in a blender container and blend until well mixed. Chill.

Put the vegetables in a steamer, being careful not to crowd them. Steam over gently boiling water until cooked yet still crisp. It takes experience to judge when the texture of the vegetable is just right: The brightening then peaking of the color is a good guide. Arrange the vegetables on a platter and let cool.

Heat 1-1/2 inches (4 cm) of oil in a wok or large skillet to about 400°F (210°C), or until almost smoking. Put the fish into the oil and fry until the skin is dark brown. Turn and fry the second side. This should take 8 to 10 minutes in all. Drain the fish on paper toweling and place on the platter with the vegetables. Serve with the sauce on the side.

GOONG YAI
Baked Lobster

In Thailand, this elaborate party dish is prepared with the magnificent fresh-water lobster native to the country.

2 small Pacific spiny lobsters (about 1-1/2 pounds or 750 g total weight)
Strips of fresh side pork (fresh bacon)
4 ounces (125 g) bean-thread noodles, soaked in warm water to soften 5 minutes and drained
2 tablespoons (30 ml) light soy sauce
2 teaspoons (10 ml) Szechwan peppercorns, toasted in a dry pan until pungent and crushed
1 teaspoon (5 ml) fish sauce *(nam bla)*
2 green onions, cut into 2-inch (5 cm) lengths
2 tablespoons (30 ml) rice wine or sake
1/4 teaspoon (1 ml) sugar
1/2 teaspoon (2 ml) monosodium glutamate (optional)
1 large slice ginger, crushed with flat side of cleaver and peeled
2 garlic cloves, crushed

Wash the lobsters well under cold running water. Place, back side down, on a cutting board, and with a heavy knife, split the lobster down the middle. Remove the stomach (sand sac) and the vein running down the tail and discard. Line a warmed Pyrex dish or earthenware dish with a 1/4-inch (6 mm) layer of side pork. Top the pork with the bean-thread noodles and then arrange the lobster halves on the noodles. Combine all the remaining ingredients and pour over the lobsters. Cover and place in a preheated 350°F (180°C) oven. Bake 20 minutes or until bean-thread noodles are transparent and sauce is bubbly. Don't overcook or lobster will toughen.

Variations Substitute 1-1/2 pounds (750 g) fresh or thawed frozen uncooked lobster tails or fresh cooked lobster tails for the whole lobsters. If using uncooked tails, increase cooking time about 10 minutes. You may also substitute 3 pounds (1.5 kg) crayfish, cooked and shelled, or 1-1/2 pounds (750 g) medium shrimp, cooked and shelled, for the lobster.

This dish may be steamed instead of baked. Place, uncovered, in a steamer and cook over gently boiling water about 15 minutes for precooked shellfish, 30 minutes for uncooked shellfish.

Poultry

GAI PAHT
Chicken with Cashews

1/4 cup (60 ml) raw whole cashews
2 tablespoons (30 ml) peanut oil
2 small dried red chili peppers, coarsely chopped
1 garlic clove, crushed
6 ounces (200 g) boned chicken breast meat,
   cut into slices 1-1/2 by 3 by 1/4 inch (4 cm
   by 8 cm by 6 mm)
1/2 cup (125 ml) well drained Thai or Chinese
   canned straw mushrooms
1/4 cup (60 ml) canned miniature corn cobs,
   well drained
1/4 cup (60 ml) chicken stock
1 tablespoon (15 ml) oyster sauce *(nahm mahn hoi)*
1/2 teaspoon (2 ml) fish sauce *(nam bla)*
1/2 teaspoon (2 ml) soy sauce
1/2 teaspoon (2 ml) sugar
1/2 teaspoon (2 ml) arrowroot, dissolved in
   1 tablespoon (15 ml) water

Toast the cashews in a 325°F (160°C) oven for about 10 minutes, or until light brown; set aside. Heat the oil in a wok or skillet, add the chili peppers and then immediately add the garlic and chicken. Stir-fry 30 seconds, then add the straw mushrooms and corn cobs and stir well. Combine the chicken stock, oyster sauce, fish sauce, soy sauce, sugar and arrowroot mixture and add to wok. Stir well, cover and cook 1 minute. Uncover and stir again until the sauce bubbles and thickens. Add the reserved cashew nuts, mix well and serve.

Variation Substitute 1/2 cup (125 ml) halved fresh mushrooms for the straw mushrooms. Add to wok with the garlic and chicken.

GAI PAHT KING
Chicken Fried with Ginger

This dish incorporates ginger root as the principal vegetable. The Thais believe that ginger strengthens the blood and aids the digestion.

4 ounces (125 g) young ginger root*
Salt
2 tablespoons (30 ml) peanut oil
2 to 4 small fresh green chili peppers or equal
    amounts green bell pepper and chili pepper,
    coarsely shredded
2 garlic cloves, crushed
6 ounces (200 g) boned chicken meat, sliced or
    coarsely shredded
2 rounded tablespoons (40 ml) *small* wood fungus,
    soaked in warm water 15 minutes and drained
1/2 teaspoon (2 ml) monosodium glutamate
    (optional)
2 tablespoons (30 ml) water
2 tablespoons (30 ml) fish sauce *(nam bla),* or
    2 teaspoons (10 ml) dark soy sauce

Peel the ginger root and shred it into matchstick-size pieces. Cover with cold salted water and let stand for 10 minutes, then drain. Heat the oil in a wok or skillet, add the chili peppers and garlic and stir-fry until pungent. Add the chicken, ginger and wood fungus and stir-fry for 1-1/2 to 2 minutes. Add all remaining ingredients, stir well, cover and cook for 30 seconds, or until chicken is done.

*These are young tender ginger root shoots with a sweet, pungent flavor; available in the market in spring and early summer.

YAHNG THAI
Thai Barbecue

These two marinades are suitable for a two-pound (1 kg) broiler chicken or young duckling, split in half or quarters or left whole. Simply combine all the ingredients, rub over the fowl and marinate overnight in the refrigerator. Barbecue over hot coals or broil in the oven until golden brown, basting with any remaining marinade.

Marinade I
3/4 cup (175 ml) coconut cream
1/2 teaspoon (3 ml) ground turmeric
1 teaspoon (5 ml) ground coriander
4 garlic cloves, crushed
1 teaspoon (5 ml) ground black pepper
1/2 teaspoon (2 to 3 ml) salt

Marinade II
2 tablespoons (30 ml) tiny vinegar-packed chili
    peppers *(siling labuyo,* Philippine), finely
    chopped
1/4 cup (60 ml) sugar
Juice of 1 medium lime
2 garlic cloves, crushed
2 tablespoons (30 ml) fish sauce *(nam bla)*

BET YAHNG
Roast Duck

One of the Thai Chinese community specialties is a barbecued tiny piglet, with crispy, glazed skin and succulent meat. In this country, a suckling pig of less than 10 pounds (5 kg) is difficult to find, but a 4- or 5-pound (2 kg) duck makes a good substitute. A duck of this size will serve four persons with another dish and steamed rice. The roast duck is served in two stages—first the crispy-skin outer layer and then the meat stir-fried with vegetables.

One 4- to 5-pound (2 kg) duck, cleaned and
   wiped dry
Steamed long-grain white rice
Oyster sauce *(nahm mahn hoi)*

Marinade
1 cup (250 ml) honey
1/4 cup (60 ml) thin soy sauce
2 tablespoons (30 ml) rice vinegar
2 garlic cloves, crushed
2 tablespoons (30 ml) mashed Chinese brown bean
   sauce *(mien see)* or
   Thai soybean condiment *(dow jeeoh dam)*
1/4 teaspoon (1 to 2 ml) five-spice powder
1/4 teaspoon (1 to 2 ml) Asian chili powder
1 teaspoon (5 ml) monosodium glutamate

Stir-fry dish
2 tablespoons (30 ml) peanut oil
1 cup (250 ml) coarsely shredded celery, parboiled
   3 minutes and drained

2 cups (500 ml) bean sprouts
Sliced duck meat
2 tablespoons (30 ml) oyster sauce
2 tablespoons (30 ml) chicken stock
1/4 teaspoon (1 ml) sugar

Combine all ingredients for the marinade and rub on duck. Using twine, hang the duck in a cool, airy place for at least 4 hours, basting inside and out with the marinade every 30 minutes or so and placing a pan underneath to catch the drippings. Hanging the duck in this manner allows the skin to dry and absorb more marinade.

Place the duck on a spit and roast over a moderately hot open charcoal fire or in a rotisserie about 40 minutes, pricking the skin during cooking to allow fat to escape. Baste periodically with any remaining marinade. The skin should be a deep brown and the meat next to the bone very rare when ready. Remove the duck from the spit and split it in half. Slice off portions of the outer skin and fat and cooked meat layer and serve with steamed rice and oyster sauce. Remove the carcass to the kitchen and slice off the remaining rare meat (about 1-1/2 cups or 375 ml), which then becomes the basis of the stir-fry dish.

To make the stir-fry, heat the oil in a wok or skillet and add the celery, bean sprouts and sliced duck meat. Stir-fry over medium-high heat 1 minute. Mix together the oyster sauce, chicken stock and sugar, add to the wok, stir well, cover and cook about 30 seconds, or until vegetables are tender. Serve with steamed rice.

Beef & Pork

RAD NA
Stir-fried Beef and Vegetables

A simple one-dish meal good served over noodles or steamed rice.

3 tablespoons (45 ml) peanut oil
1 garlic clove, crushed
1 slice ginger root, crushed with flat side of cleaver and peeled
6 ounces (200 g) beef flank steak or tenderloin, sliced 1/4 inch (6 mm) thick with the grain
4 ounces (125 g) bamboo shoots or Chinese cabbage (bok choy) or other greens, thinly sliced (optional)
1/2 cup (125 ml) well drained Thai or Chinese canned straw mushrooms
1/4 cup (50 ml) chicken stock
2 tablespoons (30 ml) oyster sauce (nahm mahn hoi)
1 tablespoon (15 ml) fish sauce (nam bla) or soy sauce
1/2 teaspoon (2 ml) sugar
1/2 teaspoon (2 ml) monosodium glutamate (optional)
1/2 teaspoon (2 ml) arrowroot, dissolved in 1 tablespoon (15 ml) water
8 ounces (250 g) fresh egg noodles (bamee), cooked in boiling water until tender, drained and cooled, or
  fresh flat rice noodles at room temperature*
1 tablespoon (15 ml) dark soy sauce

Heat 2 tablespoons (30 ml) of the oil in a wok or skillet, add the garlic, ginger, beef and optional vegetable and stir-fry just until meat is seared. Add the straw mushrooms and stir well. Combine the chicken stock, oyster sauce, fish sauce, sugar, monosodium glutamate and arrowroot mixture and add to wok. Stir well, cover and cook 1 minute. Uncover and stir again until the sauce bubbles and thickens. Remove from heat and set aside; keep warm while preparing noodles.

Heat the remaining 1 tablespoon (15 ml) of oil in a wok or skillet, add the noodles and dark soy sauce and stir-fry just until noodles are heated through, 1 to 2 minutes. Do not cook too long or they will break up. Serve the beef and vegetables over the noodles.

*Dried flat rice noodles, about 1/4 inch (6 mm) wide, may be substituted for the fresh rice noodles. Soak in warm water about 15 minutes, then drain. Stir-fry as directed. If noodles are still very firm, add 2 tablespoons (30 ml) water to the wok, cover and cook 1 minute.

Variation Substitute 1/2 cup (125 ml) sliced fresh mushrooms for the canned straw mushrooms. Add to the wok with the beef.

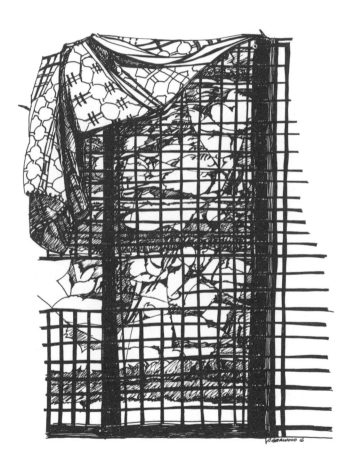

NOOUH GAP TOOUH
Beef with Peanut Sauce

1/4 cup (60 ml) raw peanuts
3/4 cup (175 ml) coconut cream
1/2 teaspoon (3 ml) soaked and crushed dried
   citrus leaf *(by maglood)* or peel *(pew maglood)*,
   or 1 teaspoon (5 ml) freshly grated lime or
   lemon rind
1/4 to 1/2 teaspoon (1 to 3 ml) Asian chili powder
2 teaspoons (10 ml) peanut oil
6 ounces (200 g) spinach leaves, coarsely shredded
6 ounces (200 g) beef round, sirloin or chuck, cut
   into strips 2 by 4 by 1/4 inch (5 cm by 10 cm
   by 6 mm)
1 teaspoon (5 ml) tamarind liquid *(som ma kham)*
   or fresh lime juice
1/4 teaspoon (1 ml) monosodium glutamate
   (optional)
1/2 teaspoon (2 ml) sugar

Toast the peanuts in a 325°F (160°C) oven for about 10 minutes, or until light brown. Grind them in a mortar or nut grinder and combine with the coconut cream, citrus leaf and chili powder in a small saucepan. Place over medium heat, stirring often, until pungent. Meanwhile, heat the oil in a wok or skillet and stir-fry the spinach just until wilted. Remove from heat and set aside. Add the beef to the coconut milk and simmer 1 minute, stirring occasionally. Add all remaining ingredients, including the spinach, and simmer about 2 minutes longer, or until beef is cooked.

PAHT BLEEOH WAN
Sweet and Sour Pork

2 tablespoons (30 ml) peanut oil
1 garlic clove, crushed
6 ounces (200 g) pork rump, shoulder or loin, sliced into pieces 1-1/2 by 4 by 1/4 inch (4 cm by 10 cm by 6 mm)
2 medium fresh green chili peppers, coarsely shredded
1/2 medium onion, coarsely shredded
1/2 cup (125 ml) pineapple chunks
1 small tomato, cut into wedges
1 tablespoon (15 ml) fish sauce *(nam bla)*
1 teaspoon (5 ml) sugar, or to taste
1/4 teaspoon (1 ml) monosodium glutamate (optional)
1 tablespoon (15 ml) water

Heat the oil in a wok or skillet, add the garlic and stir-fry until pungent. Add the pork, chili peppers and onion and stir-fry 1 minute. Add all remaining ingredients, stir well, cover and cook about 2 minutes, or until pork is done.

Variation Substitute 6 ounces (200 g) medium shrimp, shelled and deveined, for the pork. Proceed as directed in recipe, but cook only 1 minute after covering.

Note If a greater amount of sauce is desired, dissolve 1/2 teaspoon (3 ml) arrowroot in 1/4 cup (50 ml) water and add to wok just before covering. Omit the 1 tablespoon (15 ml) water.

KY YAHT SY
Sweet Pork Omelet

2 tablespoons (30 ml) plus 1 teaspoon (5 ml) peanut oil
4 ounces (125 g) ground pork
1 teaspoon (5 ml) fish sauce *(nam bla),* or 1/2 teaspoon (3 ml) dark soy sauce
1/4 teaspoon (1 ml) monosodium glutamate (optional)
1-1/2 teaspoons (7 ml) sugar
1/2 cup (125 ml) shelled green peas or chopped vegetable of choice, such as carrots or mushrooms
4 eggs, beaten

Heat 1 teaspoon of the oil in a wok or skillet and stir-fry the pork over medium-high heat 3 minutes, breaking up the lumps. Add the fish sauce or soy sauce, monosodium glutamate, sugar and vegetable and stir-fry 2 minutes, or until mixture is cooked and no liquid remains. Remove from pan and set aside to cool to room temperature.

Heat the remaining oil in an 8-inch (20 cm) skillet placed over medium-high heat. Pour in the eggs, and when they begin to set, spoon the pork mixture on one half and fold the other half over the top. Cook over medium heat, turning once, until both sides are brown, the center is fluffy and the omelet starts to puff. Remove from pan and cut in half crosswise to serve.

GADOOK MOO PAHT GATIEM PLIK TY
Spareribs with Garlic and Pepper

In this dish, the ribs are fried in oil to leach out the fat, much in the same way that the fat is released in steaming. Here, however, the ribs end up wonderfully crispy.

1-pound-slab (500 g) pork spareribs
1 tablespoon (15 ml) chopped fresh coriander
   stems
4 garlic cloves, crushed
1 teaspoon (5 ml) monosodium glutamate
   (optional)
1 teaspoon (5 ml) ground black pepper
2 teaspoons (10 ml) fish sauce *(nam bla),* or to
   taste
Peanut oil for deep-frying

Select spareribs that are small so that they may be left whole. Cut the slab into individual ribs. Combine all remaining ingredients except oil and marinate the spareribs in the mixture at least 20 minutes. (If you have time, marinate a few hours or overnight, refrigerated.)

Heat the oil to a depth of 2 inches (5 cm) in a wok or skillet until very hot. Add spareribs to wok and cook about 6 minutes on each side, or until dark brown. Remove spareribs from the oil with a slotted utensil and serve.

MOO PAHT GATIEM PLIK TY
Pork with Garlic and Pepper

6 ounces (200 g) pork shoulder or rump, cut into
   slices 2 by 4 by 1/2 inch (5 by 10 by 1.5 cm)
1 tablespoon (15 ml) chopped fresh coriander
   stems
4 garlic cloves, crushed
1 teaspoon (5 ml) monosodium glutamate
   (optional)
1 teaspoon (5 ml) ground black pepper
2 teaspoons (10 ml) fish sauce *(nam bla),* or to
   taste
Peanut oil
1 small onion, cut into 1/2-inch-thick (1.5 cm)
   slices
1 small tomato, cut into 1/2-inch (1.5 cm) dice

Combine the pork, coriander, garlic, monosodium glutamate, pepper and fish sauce and marinate at least 20 minutes. (If you have time, marinate a few hours or overnight, refrigerated.)

Heat the oil to a depth of 3/4 inch (2 cm) in a wok or skillet until very hot. Add pork slices to wok and cook about 3 minutes on each side, or until dark brown. Pour off almost all of the oil, add the onion and stir-fry 30 seconds. Add the tomato, stir well, cover and cook 30 to 60 seconds.

SATAY
Shish Kabob

For pork satay

8 ounces (250 g) pork shoulder or butt, cut into
   strips 1 by 4 by 1/2 inch (3 by 10 by 1.5 cm)
1/4 cup (60 ml) coconut cream
1 teaspoon (5 ml) ground coriander
1/2 teaspoon (2 ml) ground turmeric

For shrimp or fish satay

8 ounces (250 g) medium shrimp, shelled and
   deveined, or firm fresh fish fillets, cut into
   1-1/2-inch (4 cm) squares
2 tablespoons (30 ml) rich chicken stock
2 teaspoons (10 ml) rice wine or dry sherry
1 tablespoon (15 ml) chopped fresh mint
1 teaspoon (5 ml) ground black pepper

Satay sauce

3/4 cup (200 ml) raw peanuts
1-1/2 cups (375 ml) coconut cream
1 small dried red chili pepper, finely chopped
2 tablespoons (30 ml) tamarind liquid *(som
   ma kham)* or fresh lime juice
1 teaspoon (5 ml) fish sauce *(nam bla)*
1/2 teaspoon (3 ml) ground lemon grass
   (da kry)
1/4 to 1/2 cup (60 to 125 ml) water
2 to 4 tablespoons (30 to 60 ml) sugar

Cucumbers

1 large cucumber, peeled and sliced 1/8 to 1/4
   inch (3 to 6 mm) thick
1 tablespoon (15 ml) rice vinegar

1 tablespoon (15 ml) water
1/2 small red onion, sliced
1/4 teaspoon (1 ml) salt
1/4 teaspoon (1 ml) sugar
1 small fresh green chili pepper, shredded

Combine the pork with its marinade ingredients or
the shrimp or fish with its marinade ingredients
and let stand for at least 30 minutes. Soak 6 to 10
bamboo skewers (about 10 inches or 25 cm in
length) in water.

To prepare the sauce, toast the peanuts in an
oven preheated to 325°F (160°C) about 10
minutes, or until light brown. Grind them in a
mortar or nut grinder and set aside. Combine the
coconut cream and chili pepper in a saucepan and
place over medium-high heat until pungent, stirring
often. Add the ground peanuts, tamarind liquid or
lime juice, fish sauce, lemon grass, water and sugar
to the coconut cream and simmer, uncovered, 30
minutes or until thick, stirring often.

To prepare the cucumbers, combine all
ingredients and let stand at least 10 minutes for
flavors to blend.

Remove the skewers from the water and thread
2 to 3 pork slices, shrimp or fish cubes on each.
Grill the pork over hot charcoal about 3 minutes
on each side, or until golden and seared on the
outside, yet tender on the inside. The shrimp and
fish will take less cooking time; watch them
carefully so they do not overcook. Serve the *satay*
with the sauce and cucumbers on the side.

Sweets

COW NEEOH MIMAWN
Sticky Rice with Mangoes

This light dessert is a fruity, creamy type of rice pudding.

2 cups (500 ml) glutinous rice *(cow neeoh)*
1/4 cup (60 ml) sugar
1/2 teaspoon (2 ml) salt
3/4 cup (200 ml) coconut cream
1 large mango, peeled, pitted and sliced

Soak the rice in hot tap water to cover 1 hour. Drain and put in a vessel to be set in a steamer. Steam the rice over simmering water until soft and sticky but not mushy, about 1-1/2 to 2 hours. To test for doneness, press kernels between fingertips; if there is no firm core, the rice is cooked. Remove from steamer and mix in the sugar, salt and half the coconut cream. Let cool to room temperature. Serve on a platter, crowned with mango slices and the remaining coconut cream poured over the top.

Variations Substitute whipped heavy cream or canned sweetened condensed milk for the coconut cream topping.

BEEYAK CAHMPOHT
Creamed Corn

2 young ears corn, or
    3/4 cup (200 ml) frozen corn kernels
1/2 cup (125 ml) water
1/2 cup (125 ml) sugar
1/4 teaspoon (1 ml) salt
1/2 cup (125 ml) coconut cream
2 tablespoons (30 ml) freshly grated coconut meat
    or unsweetened dried grated coconut

Cut the kernels from the corn cobs with a sharp knife. Combine the kernels, water, sugar and salt in a saucepan and cook, stirring frequently, over medium heat 5 minutes, or until the corn is tender and the liquid is syrupy. Remove from the heat and chill. Just before serving, stir in the coconut cream and top with grated coconut.

CUTTING A PINEAPPLE, THAI STYLE

The Thais have a very artistic way of serving a pineapple that actually is much simpler to do than the impressive result would make one think.

Begin by holding the pineapple, stem end up, on a flat hard surface, such as a cutting board. With a medium-length knife, slice off the skin in strong, even strokes from the top to the bottom of the pineapple. Be careful to cut off only the skin without taking any of the precious meat. The bumps or "eyes" of the pineapple, which are arranged in a geometrical, circular pattern, should be clearly visible. Lay the pineapple on its side, and with the point of a sharp knife, cut out the eyes, usually three at a time, by following their course around the body of the pineapple in a continuous spiral. When you have removed the eyes, the pineapple will have a spiral "groove" that covers its entire surface. The pineapple is traditionally served with salt.

SAKOO
Tapioca with Water Chestnuts

2 cups (500 ml) water
1/3 cup (75 ml) quick-cooking tapioca
1/4 cup (60 ml) coconut cream
2 tablespoons (30 ml) sugar
1/4 teaspoon (1 ml) salt
1/4 cup (60 ml) fresh corn kernels
6 fresh water chestnuts, peeled and sliced

Coconut cream topping
1/2 cup (125 ml) coconut cream
1 tablespoon (15 ml) sugar
1 teaspoon (5 ml) regular rice flour
1/8 teaspoon (0.5 ml) salt

Bring the water to a boil in a saucepan and stir in the tapioca. Lower heat until mixture barely simmers and cook, stirring, 3 minutes. Remove from heat; the tapioca should not be quite cooked. Mix in the coconut cream, sugar, salt and corn, and set aside.

Mix together all the ingredients for the coconut cream topping in a small saucepan and place over medium heat. Simmer, stirring frequently, 2 minutes or until slightly thickened. Divide the water chestnut slices evenly between 6 1/2-cup (125 ml) custard cups. Pour one sixth of the tapioca mixture into each cup and then top with one sixth of the coconut cream topping. Place the custard cups in a steamer and steam over gently boiling water 15 minutes or until set. Remove from steamer and let cool slightly before serving so that tapioca jells completely.

GLOOAY TAWT
Fried Bananas

4 ripe, firm bananas
Peanut oil for deep-frying

Batter
1 cup (250 ml) water
1 cup (250 ml) regular rice flour
1 egg, beaten (optional)
1/2 teaspoon (2 ml) salt
1/4 cup (60 ml) sesame seeds
2 tablespoons (30 ml) finely shredded fresh
    coconut meat or unsweetened dried coconut

To prepare the batter, combine all the ingredients and mix just enough to moisten the dry ingredients. Do not overmix; the batter should remain lumpy. Chill well.

When you are ready to cook the bananas, heat about 2 inches (5 cm) of oil in a wok or deep skillet to 375°F (190°C). Peel the bananas and slice them on the diagonal 3/4 inch (2 cm) thick. Dip the banana slices in the batter and deep-fry them, a few pieces at a time, for 30 seconds, or until golden brown and crispy.

Variations Substitute 1 sweet potato or medium taro root, peeled and cut in 1/2-inch-thick (1.5 cm) semicircles for the banana. Proceed as directed.

The Thais also make a type of peanut brittle using this same batter. Mix 2 cups (500 ml) raw peanuts into the batter. Cook the batter in batches in hot oil until it forms a golden brown mass.

COW TAWM PAHT
Sticky Rice Dumplings

2 cups (500 ml) glutinous rice *(cow neeoh)*
3/4 cup (200 ml) coconut cream
1 teaspoon (5 ml) sugar
1/2 teaspoon (2 ml) salt
2 medium bananas, finely diced, or
   1 can (9 ounce or 255 g) Chinese sweet red bean
   paste

Soak the rice in hot tap water to cover 1 hour. Drain well, mix in coconut cream, sugar and salt and cook, stirring frequently, over medium heat until the rice is half cooked, about 10 minutes. Remove from heat and let rice cool enough to handle. Take a handful of the rice, shape into a ball and make an indentation in the center. Fill the indentation with the filling of your choice, then press the rice together so that the filling is completely encased in the center of the ball. Repeat with remaining rice and filling. Wrap each dumpling in aluminum foil and place them, without crowding, in a steamer. Steam over gently boiling water 40 minutes to 1 hour, or until rice is soft. Alternately, place the foil packages on a grill above a slow charcoal fire and, turning occasionally, cook about 30 minutes.

Note In a more traditional preparation, the dumplings are wrapped in large pieces of banana leaf rather than foil. Scald the leaves or hold them over heat to make them pliable. Place each dumpling in the center of a leaf and fold in the sides to make a secure bundle. Fasten closed with bamboo skewers, wooden picks or heavy thread, then steam or cook over charcoal as directed.

KANOME PUAK GOOWUM
Taro Root Candy

1 pound (500 g) taro root, peeled and cut into
   1/2-inch (1.5 cm) cubes
1 cup (250 ml) coconut cream
2 cups (500 ml) sugar
2 cups (500 ml) water

Combine all ingredients in a saucepan and simmer, uncovered, 40 minutes to 1 hour, or until reduced to a sticky, syrupy, but not crystallized, mass. Keep stirring the mixture and mashing the taro root throughout the cooking process. The taro root should be completely dispersed through the syrup, without any stuck to the saucepan, when the mixture is ready.

Wipe a 1-quart (1 L) baking dish with peanut-oil soaked paper toweling (or use a nonstick pan) and pour in the hot taro mixture. Let cool and cut into squares to serve. Store this taffylike candy in a cool place or in the refrigerator.

Variation Substitute 1 pound (500 g) yams, peeled and cut as directed, for the taro root.

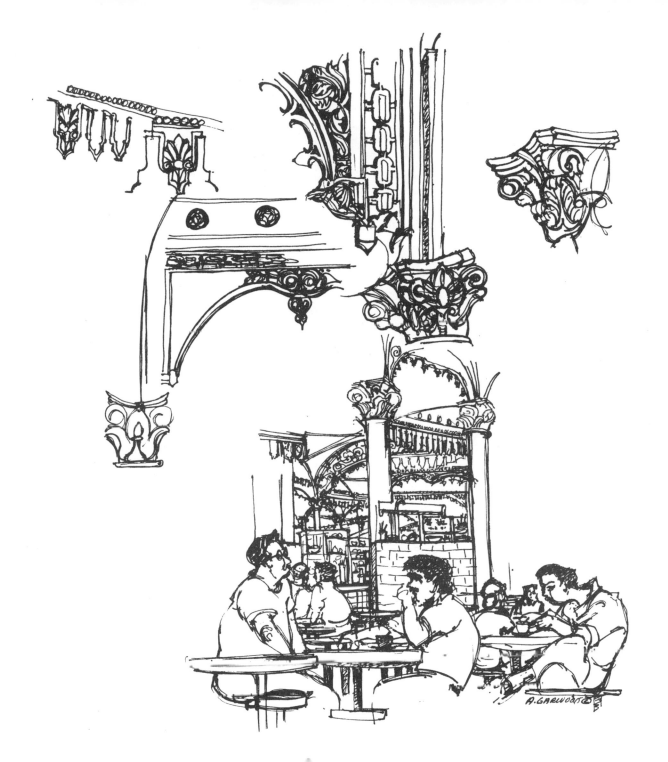

KANOME
Jelled Dessert

A wide variety of jelled sweets are sold from street-side stands throughout Thailand. These colorful, cool desserts are especially good in hot weather. They are made with agar-agar, a thickening agent derived from seaweed. Agar-agar is most commonly available in two forms: sheets of translucent strands most easily found in Japanese markets under the name *kanten,* or powder, available in Chinese groceries and pharmacies. Agar-agar can also be found in some health-food stores.

1/4 ounce (7 g) agar-agar strands
2-1/2 to 3 cups (625 to 750 ml) hot water
1 cup (250 ml) sugar
Few drops food coloring of choice
Flavoring of choice: juice of 1/2 medium lime or
   1/4 teaspoon (1 to 2 ml) vanilla or almond
   extract
3/4 cup (200 ml) coconut cream
1/2 teaspoon (2 ml) regular rice flour
1/4 teaspoon (1 ml) salt
1/2 cup (125 ml) unsweetened dried grated
   coconut

Soak the agar-agar in the hot water 30 minutes. Combine the agar-agar, soaking water and sugar in a saucepan and place over medium heat. Simmer 10 minutes, stirring frequently. Stir in food coloring and flavoring of choice and pour into a flat tray to a depth of 3/4 to 1 inch (2 to 3 cm). Chill mixture until firm.

Meanwhile, combine the coconut cream, rice flour and salt in a saucepan and place over medium heat. Simmer a few minutes until thickened. Remove from heat and let cool to room temperature, then pour over the set "jelly" and chill thoroughly. Top with grated coconut and cut into squares to serve.

Variations One-half-inch (1.5 cm) cubes of cooked taro root or sweet potato or sliced fresh water chestnuts may be added to the agar-agar mixture with the food coloring and flavoring.

FOI TAWNG KROB
Golden Silk

1-1/2 cups (375 ml) sugar
1 cup (250 ml) water
6 medium egg yolks, lightly beaten

Combine the sugar and water in a saucepan and place over medium-high heat, stirring constantly, until syrupy and the soft-ball stage is reached (240°F or 115°C). Using a metal funnel, stiff-paper cone or pastry bag and nozzle, very slowly add the egg yolk in a *fine, steady stream,* forming circles. In 2 to 3 minutes, the strands will have set and can be gently removed with chopsticks and piled on a plate to cool.

VIETNAM

The Vietnamese Meal

There is much talk of the influence of the Chinese and the French on the cuisine of Vietnam, and though the mark of these two cuisines cannot be ignored, true Vietnamese food has its own character and taste.

All kinds of meat—pork, beef, chicken and duck—are eaten in Vietnam, but pork is the most popular because it costs the least. Duck is also popular, and unlike in the United States, is less expensive than chicken. Lamb is generally served only at restaurants. Fresh-and-salt-water fish and shellfish are eaten more than any kind of meat, however, because of their abundance. Raw vegetables, mostly in the form of simple salads, and fruit are popular.

There are generally three meals a day, and rice is a must at two of them. At family meals, all of the dishes are served at once. They are placed in the center of the table and eaten from communally. If a guest or guests are present, however, the dishes are usually served one at a time.

Pho, a hearty rice-noodle soup, is popularly eaten for breakfast. French bread with luncheon meat, borrowed from the French, and glutinous rice are also common breakfast fare. Lunch and dinner are equivalent in size in Vietnam, unlike in the United States where lunch is a much lighter meal. The table is set with small bowls and chopsticks and a typical meal would consist of a soup, rice, a vegetable or salad and a salty fish or meat dish. Hot tea is usually served at the end of the meal, though on special occasions soft drinks are served to the women and children and the men are served Western wine and liquor or beer in the populated areas and locally made rice wine in the rural areas. Sweets are generally not served at the end of meals, but rather taken during the day as snacks. Fresh fruit, such as bananas, papaya, pineapples and mangoes, are often served at the conclusion of the meal.

ABOUT THE RECIPES

Most of the recipes that follow will serve four persons when combined with another dish and a soup, unless otherwise specified. You, of course, may halve the recipes or increase them according to the number of diners.

The dishes presented here are northern Vietnamese in origin and are those that might be eaten in a middle class home. You will see the influence of the French, and to a lesser degree the Chinese, in the recipes, though this refinement is mainly confined to urban areas.

Readers should use these recipes as guidelines for their own experimentation. The amount of any ingredient can be increased or decreased as desired. The addition of the ever-present fish sauce *(nuoc mam),* the most important flavoring in Vietnamese cuisine, may take some getting used to by uninitiated palates. The secret is to add some of this pungent, salty sauce, taste the result, add some more, taste again and continue until it tastes good to you. Chili peppers (red or green, fresh or dried, may be used) and garlic, though commonly used, are indicated optional in many recipes. The dish will taste fine without them, though it will taste better with them. Even the fish sauce can be replaced with salt or soy sauce (the latter in a greater measure than the fish sauce) if you find its pungency objectionable. You should, however, try the traditional seasonings to get an accurate sense of Vietnamese food.

A note about two ingredients: Monosodium glutamate, though frequently used in urban areas, is rarely used by people in the countryside in Vietnam. Its presence in the following recipes is because of this urban use and it can be omitted without any fear of ruining the dish. In contrast, the use of garlic powder is a purely American invention. I have found its flavor is absorbed into meats more completely and quickly during marination than fresh cloves. Fresh garlic can, however, be substituted for the powder.

Rice & Noodles

XOI GA
Glutinous Rice and Chicken

2 cups (500 ml) glutinous rice
1 cup (250 ml) mung dhal (dried mung bean
   halves without skin)
1/2 teaspoon (3 ml) salt
5 ounces (150 g) chicken meat, finely chopped
1 tablespoon (15 ml) fish sauce *(nuoc mam)*

Wash rice and mung beans in water several times until the water is clear. Put the rice and beans and salt in a pot and add cold water to cover the rice by 1/4 inch (6 mm). Put the pot over high heat and cook, uncovered, until all of the water has evaporated from the surface of the rice. Put the pot in a preheated 325°F (160°C) oven for about 20 minutes. While the rice is cooking, stir-fry the chicken and fish sauce in a wok or skillet until chicken is tender. Remove the rice from the oven and check for doneness. The rice kernels should be transparent and the mung beans should be easily crushed with your fingertips. Stir the chicken into rice and serve.

Note This dish may also be steamed. Soak the rice and beans in water to cover 4 hours. Drain and wash rice and beans until water runs clear. Transfer to a steamer and steam above gently boiling water 35 to 45 minutes, or until kernels are transparent and beans can be easily crushed with your fingertips. Prepare chicken as directed and stir into rice.

COM CHIEN
Fried Rice

4 tablespoons (60 ml) peanut oil
4 shallots, thinly sliced
4 ounces (125 g) chicken meat, beef, pork or
   shelled shrimp, finely chopped, or a combination
1 cup (250 ml) shelled green peas or chopped
   green beans
4 tablespoons (60 ml) fish sauce *(nuoc mam)*
6 cups (1.5 L) cold cooked rice
Ground black pepper

Heat 2 tablespoons (30 ml) of the oil in a wok or skillet, add half of the shallots and stir-fry until golden. Add the meat, vegetables and 2 tablespoons (30 ml) of the fish sauce and stir-fry until meat and vegetables are tender. Remove from the pan and set aside. Heat the remaining 2 tablespoons (60 ml) oil in the pan, add the remaining shallots and stir-fry until golden. Add the rice and remaining 2 tablespoons (30 ml) fish sauce and stir-fry until rice seems dry. Return the meat and vegetables to the pan and stir-fry 2 minutes. Transfer to a serving dish and sprinkle with black pepper.

CHA GIO
Egg Rolls

Also commonly called imperial rolls, egg rolls are especially good when filled with shrimp and crab meat. They may also be filled with ground chicken or pork, or any combination of the above ingredients. You will hopefully be able to obtain the rice paper wrappers, large, paper-thin, translucent rounds made of rice flour and water, that are traditionally used by the Vietnamese. If not, spring roll skins (available at Chinese markets) or *lumpia* skins (available at Philippine markets) may be substituted.

The egg rolls can be made a day ahead of time and refrigerated, then cooked just before serving. They can be served as an hors d'oeuvre or a main dish with a side dish of carrots, turnips and onions. This recipe will serve 12 persons as a main dish.

2-1/2 pounds (1.25 kg) shrimp, shelled and
    deveined
12 ounces (375 g) crab meat

10 large wood fungus or 1/4 cup (60 ml) small
    ones, soaked in warm water 30 minutes,
    drained and very thinly sliced
2 ounces (60 g) bean-thread noodles, soaked in
    warm water 30 minutes, drained and cut into
    1/2-inch (1.5 cm) lengths
2 medium onions, finely chopped
5 shallots, finely chopped
1/2 teaspoon (3 ml) ground black pepper
4 tablespoons (60 ml) fish sauce *(nuoc mam)*
2 eggs, beaten
40 rice paper wrappers
Beer or water
Peanut oil for deep-frying

Nuoc mam sauce
2 tablespoons (30 ml) water
2 tablespoons (30 ml) distilled white vinegar
1 tablespoon (15 ml) sugar
3 tablespoons (45 ml) fish sauce *(nuoc mam)*
1/2 teaspoon (3 ml) finely chopped garlic, or
    to taste
1/2 teaspoon (3 ml) finely chopped fresh red
    chili pepper, or to taste

Carrots, turnips and onions
2 carrots, peeled and cut into thin rounds or
    rectangular pieces about 1-1/2 inches (4 cm)
    long and 1 inch (3 cm) wide
2 turnips, peeled and cut into rounds or
    rectangular pieces about 1-1/2 inches (4 cm)
    long and 1 inch (3 cm) wide
2 medium onions, thinly sliced lengthwise
2 tablespoons (30 ml) sugar
6 tablespoons (90 ml) distilled white vinegar
6 tablespoons (90 ml) water

Grind or finely mince the shrimp. Combine with the crab meat, wood fungus, bean-thread noodles, onions, shallots, black pepper and fish sauce and mix well. Add the eggs and mix in well with chopsticks or a fork.

To form the rolls, lay one of the rice paper rounds on a tray or flat plate. Brush it well with beer or water so that it is pliable enough to fold. (You can moisten 2 or 3 sheets at a time to speed the process of making the rolls.) Place about 1-1/2 tablespoons (22 ml) of the filling in the center of the bottom third of the round. (See page 153.) Fold the end nearest you over the filling, then fold in the sides and roll up jelly-roll fashion. Repeat with remaining wrappers and filling. If you prefer to make smaller rolls, cut the rice paper rounds into quarters. Use only about 1-1/2 teaspoons (7 ml) filling for each quarter and roll up jelly-roll fashion from the rounded end. Set aside.

To make the *nuoc mam* sauce, combine all the ingredients, stirring well to dissolve the sugar. To prepare the vegetables, combine the carrots, turnips and onions in a bowl. Mix together the sugar, vinegar and water, stirring well to dissolve the sugar, and pour over the vegetables.

Heat oil to a depth of about 2 inches (5 cm) until very hot (about 375°F or 190°C). Deep-fry a few of the rolls at a time until crisp and golden. Serve immediately with *nuoc mam* sauce for dipping and the vegetables on the side.

Note The Vietnamese often serve these rolls with lettuce leaves and sprigs of coriander and a variety of mint. The diner wraps the roll in a lettuce leaf and tucks in a few of the herb sprigs before dipping in the *nuoc mam* sauce.

BUN BO XAO
Beef with Rice Vermicelli

1 pound (500 g) beef flank steak or other tender cut, cut against the grain into slices 1-1/2 by 1 by 1/8 inch (4 cm by 3 cm by 3 mm)
2 tablespoons (30 ml) fish sauce *(nuoc mam)*
1/4 teaspoon (1 to 2 ml) garlic powder
1/4 teaspoon (1 to 2 ml) ground black pepper
Carrots and turnips (page 138)
Nuoc mam sauce (page 138)
1 tablespoon (15 ml) salt
4 tablespoons (60 ml) peanut oil
8 ounces (250 g) rice vermicelli *(bun)*
2 garlic cloves, crushed
2 onions, sliced lengthwise
1/2 head iceberg lettuce, thinly shredded
1/4 cup (60 ml) unsalted roasted peanuts, crushed

Combine the beef, fish sauce, garlic powder and black pepper and let stand 30 minutes. Prepare the turnips and carrots and *nuoc mam* sauce and set aside.

Bring a large pot of water to a boil and add the salt and 1 tablespoon (15 ml) of the peanut oil. Add the rice vermicelli and cook just until tender, 6 to 8 minutes. Drain well. While the noodles are cooking, heat the remaining 3 tablespoons (45 ml) peanut oil in a wok or skillet and brown the garlic cloves. Discard the garlic, add the beef and onion to the pan and stir-fry until beef is browned.

Divide the vermicelli evenly among 4 bowls. Top them with the lettuce, carrots and turnips, beef and then the crushed peanuts. Each diner adds *nuoc mam* sauce to taste.

BUN THIT NUONG
Charcoal-broiled Pork and Rice Vermicelli

1 pound (500 g) pork shoulder, cut against the
    grain into slices 1-1/2 by 1 by 1/16 inch (4 cm
    by 3 cm by 1.5 mm)
4 shallots, thinly sliced
2 tablespoons (30 ml) fish sauce *(nuoc mam)*
1/4 teaspoon (1 to 2 ml) garlic powder
1/4 teaspoon (1 to 2 ml) ground black pepper
2 tablespoons (30 ml) lard or peanut oil
Carrots and turnips (page 138)
Nuoc mam sauce (page 138)
1 tablespoon (15 ml) salt
1 tablespoon (15 ml) peanut oil
8 ounces (250 g) rice vermicelli *(bun)*

Combine the pork, shallots, fish sauce, garlic powder and black pepper. Heat 2 tablespoons (30 ml)
lard or oil in a small pan until hot and pour it over
the meat mixture. Mix lightly and let stand 1 hour.
Prepare the carrots and turnips and the *nuoc mam*
sauce and set aside.

Arrange the meat on a grill over a charcoal fire
and cook until browned, turning once. While the
meat is cooking, bring a large pot of water to a boil
and add the salt and 1 tablespoon (15 ml) peanut
oil. Add the rice vermicelli and cook just until
tender, 6 to 8 minutes. Drain well and divide the
vermicelli evenly among 4 bowls. Top the noodles
with the pork and serve. Each diner adds the vegetables and *nuoc mam* sauce to his bowl as desired.

Note The pork may also be arranged on a baking
sheet and cooked in a 300°F (150°C) oven 20 to 25
minutes.

GA XAO MIEN
Fried Chicken and Bean-Thread Noodles

8 ounces (250 g) boned chicken meat, cut into
    1/2-inch (1.5 cm) pieces
2 tablespoons (30 ml) fish sauce *(nuoc mam)*
1 small onion, sliced lengthwise
1/8 teaspoon (1 ml) ground black pepper
5 tablespoons (75 ml) peanut oil
8 ounces (250 g) bean-thread noodles *(mien)*,
    soaked in warm water to soften and cut
    into 3-inch (8 cm) lengths
1 cup (250 ml) water
Fish sauce *(nuoc mam)*, ground black pepper and
    chopped fresh coriander to taste

Combine the chicken, 1 tablespoon (15 ml) of the
fish sauce, the onion and pepper and let stand 30
minutes. Heat the oil in a wok or skillet, add the
chicken and stir-fry about 2 minutes. Add the
bean-thread noodles, remaining 1 tablespoon (15
ml) fish sauce and water and cook, stirring constantly, until bean threads are transparent and the
liquid is absorbed. Season to taste with fish sauce.
Transfer to a serving dish and sprinkle with black
pepper and coriander.

Variations Substitute 8 ounces (250 g) chicken
gizzards and livers, cut into 1/2-inch (1.5 cm)
pieces, for the chicken meat. Stir-fry the gizzards
about 1 minute before adding the livers. Proceed as
directed in the recipe.

Eight ounces (250 g) crab meat may also be
substituted for the chicken meat. Proceed as directed in the recipe, but add the crab meat when
the bean-thread noodles just start to become clear.

Vegetables & Salads

RAU XAO
Stir-fried Vegetables

Vegetable oil
2 fresh bean curd cakes, cut crosswise into 1/2-
    inch-thick (1.5 cm) strips
1 small head cauliflower, broken into small
    flowerets
2 tablespoons (30 ml) water
3 ounces (90 g) fresh mushrooms, sliced
Ground black pepper to taste
Salt or thin soy sauce to taste
Chopped fresh coriander

Heat the oil in a wok or skillet to a depth of about
2 inches (5 cm) and deep-fry the bean curd until
lightly golden. Remove the bean curd with a
slotted utensil and drain on paper toweling. Pour
off all but 2 tablespoons (30 ml) of the oil and
heat oil remaining in pan until very hot. Add the
cauliflower and water and stir-fry for a few minutes. Add the mushrooms and stir-fry 1 minute.
Add the bean curd and salt or soy sauce to taste.
Transfer to a serving dish and sprinkle with black
pepper and coriander.

GOI TOM THIT
Pork, Shrimp and Vegetable Salad

4 ounces (125 g) pork shoulder
4 ounces (125 g) shrimp, shelled and deveined
2 cups (500 ml) matchstick-cut carrots
2 cups (500 ml) matchstick-cut icicle radish
    (daikon)
1 cup (250 ml) matchstick-cut cucumber
2 teaspoons (10 ml) salt

Sauce
3 tablespoons (45 ml) fish sauce (nuoc mam)
2 tablespoons (30 ml) distilled white vinegar
2 tablespoons (30 ml) sugar
1/2 teaspoon (3 ml) finely chopped garlic
Chopped fresh chili pepper to taste (optional)

Boil the pork and shrimp separately in water to
cover until tender. Drain and thinly slice pork and
cut shrimp in half lengthwise; set aside. Combine
the carrots, radish and cucumber with salt and let
stand 10 minutes. Rinse the salt off with water and
drain well; set aside. Combine all of the ingredients
for the sauce and stir well to dissolve the sugar.
Combine the vegetables, pork and shrimp and toss
to mix. Pour two thirds of the sauce over the salad
and mix thoroughly. Use the remaining sauce for
dipping the salad into as it is eaten.

GA XE PHAY
Chicken and Cabbage Salad

3 chicken thighs
4 cups (1 L) shredded cabbage
1 small onion, thinly sliced lengthwise
1/2 cup (125 ml) matchstick-cut carrot

Sauce
2 tablespoons (30 ml) fish sauce *(nuoc mam)*
2 teaspoons (10 ml) distilled white vinegar
4 teaspoons (20 ml) sugar
1/4 teaspoon (1 to 2 ml) finely chopped garlic
Chopped fresh chili pepper to taste (optional)

Cook the chicken thighs in boiling water to cover until tender; drain and let cool. Bone the chicken and cut it into thin strips; set aside. Combine all of the ingredients for the sauce and stir well to dissolve the sugar. Combine the chicken, cabbage, onion and carrot and mix with one half of the sauce. Use the remaining sauce for dipping the salad into as it is eaten.

DUA CAI
Pickled Mustard Greens

1 pound (500 g) mustard greens
3 tablespoons (45 ml) salt
2 tablespoons (30 ml) sugar
2 quarts (2 L) water

Cut mustard greens crosswise into pieces 1/2 inch (1.5 cm) wide and 2 inches (5 cm) long. Wash well and set aside. Mix the salt and sugar into the water in a large wide-mouthed jar. Add the vegetable to the solution, making sure that the water covers it completely. (A small dish can be used to weight down the vegetable to keep it from floating.) Cover loosely and let stand at room temperature until the mustard turns yellow, about 4 to 5 days. Drain and serve with Thit Kho Nuoc Dua (page 144).

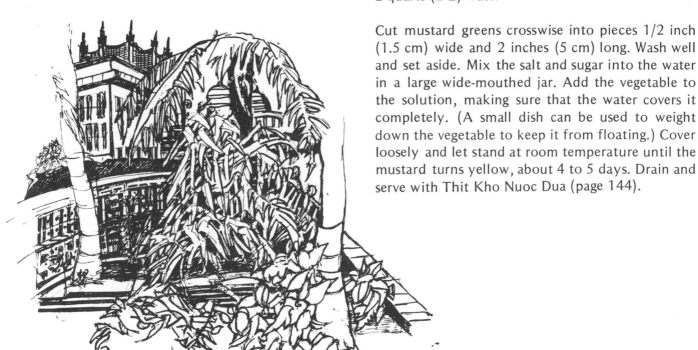

Soups

CANH CHUA
Sour Fish Soup

1 pound (500 g) snapper, or fish of choice, cut
    into 6 pieces
2 tablespoons (30 ml) fish sauce *(nuoc mam)*
1 onion, sliced lengthwise
2 quarts (2 L) water
2 teaspoons (10 ml) tamarind liquid
4 tomatoes, sliced lengthwise
2 cups (500 ml) bean sprouts
1 cup (250 ml) diagonally sliced celery
Fish sauce *(nuoc mam)* to taste
Fresh red chili pepper slices (optional)
Ground black pepper

Combine the fish, fish sauce and onion in a saucepan and cook for a few minutes over medium heat.
Add the water and tamarind liquid, bring to a boil,
reduce heat, cover and simmer about 30 minutes.
Return the soup to the boil and add the tomatoes.
When the tomatoes just begin to soften, add the
bean sprouts and celery. Season to taste with fish
sauce and chili pepper. Bring to a boil, remove
from heat and sprinkle with pepper just before
serving.

Variation Add 1 cup (250 ml) sliced pineapple
when adding the tomatoes.

CA NAU CA CHUA
Fish and Tomato Soup

Dill is commonly used to flavor fish dishes in
northern Vietnam.

1 tablespoon (15 ml) peanut oil
1 pound (500 g) white fish of choice, such as bass,
    cod, snapper, cut into 6 pieces
4 medium tomatoes, sliced lengthwise
1 onion, sliced lengthwise
2 tablespoons (30 ml) fish sauce *(nuoc mam)*
2 quarts (2 L) water
Fish sauce *(nuoc mam)* to taste
1 to 2 celery stalks, cut on the diagonal into
    1-inch (3 cm) pieces
1 tablespoon (15 ml) minced fresh dill, or
    1 teaspoon (5 ml) dried dill
Ground black pepper

Heat the oil in a wok or skillet and lightly brown
the fish pieces. Combine the fried fish, tomatoes,
onion and fish sauce in a saucepan and cook for a
few minutes until the tomatoes are soft. Add the
water and simmer, covered, 30 minutes. Season to
taste with fish sauce. Add the celery, bring to a
boil and boil 1 minute. Add the dill and sprinkle
with black pepper.

CANH THIT CA CHUA TRUNG
Pork, Tomatoes and Egg Soup

4 ounces (125 g) pork shoulder, thinly sliced
3 tablespoons (45 ml) fish sauce (nuoc mam)
1 onion, sliced lengthwise
4 medium tomatoes, sliced lengthwise
2 quarts (2 L) water
1 teaspoon (5 ml) monosodium glutamate
   (optional)
Fish sauce (nuoc mam) to taste
2 eggs, beaten
Ground black pepper

Combine the pork, fish sauce, onion and tomatoes in a saucepan and cook for a few minutes over medium heat. Add the water and simmer, covered, 30 minutes. Add the monosodium glutamate and season to taste with fish sauce. Bring to a boil and slowly pour in the beaten eggs, stirring them into the soup with a fork or chopsticks. Continue stirring until eggs have set, then remove the soup from the heat and sprinkle with black pepper.

CANH GA
Chicken and Vegetable Soup

1 pound (500 g) chicken thighs or drumsticks
2 tablespoons (30 ml) fish sauce (nuoc mam)
10 cups (2.5 L) water
1 teaspoon (5 ml) monosodium glutamate
   (optional)
1 teaspoon (5 ml) grated ginger root
3 turnips, peeled and cut into 1-1/2-inch (4 cm)
   pieces
1/2 medium head Chinese cabbage (bok choy) or
   greens of choice, coarsely shredded on the
   diagonal
Fish sauce (nuoc mam) and ground black pepper to
taste

Bone the chicken and slice the meat into small pieces. Combine the chicken meat and bones and the fish sauce in a saucepan and cook for a few minutes over medium heat. Add the water, monosodium glutamate and ginger and simmer, covered, 30 to 40 minutes. Pick out the chicken bones and discard, then add the turnips and simmer until almost tender. Add the cabbage, bring to a boil and season to taste with fish sauce. Sprinkle with black pepper just before serving. This will serve 6.

Variation Substitute 3 ounces (90 g) fresh mushrooms, sliced, for the turnips. Proceed as directed in the recipe.

The soups that follow can be served as a complete meal, or as one course of a large meal. They are not, however, served with rice, unlike those soups that precede them.

VIT XAO MANG
Duck and Dried Bamboo Shoot Soup

8 quarts (8 L) water
4 ounces (125 g) dried bamboo shoots*
One 4-pound (2 kg) duck, cut into serving pieces
4 tablespoons (60 ml) fish sauce *(nuoc mam)*
2 teaspoons (10 ml) monosodium glutamate
   (optional)
2 teaspoons (10 ml) grated ginger root
Fish sauce *(nuoc mam)* to taste
1/2 head lettuce, sliced
6 green onions, chopped
4 tablespoons (60 ml) chopped fresh coriander
Ground black pepper

Bring 3 quarts (3 L) of the water to a boil in a large saucepan and add the dried bamboo shoots. Boil, uncovered, for 30 minutes, then drain in a colander. Cut the bamboo shoots into 3-inch (8 cm) pieces and set aside. In the same pot, combine the duck and fish sauce and cook for a few minutes over medium heat. Add the remaining 5 quarts (5 L) water and bring to a boil. Skim all residue that forms on the surface. Add the bamboo shoots and monosodium glutamate and simmer, uncovered, for 2 hours, or until duck and bamboo shoots are tender. Season to taste with fish sauce and ladle the soup into 4 to 6 bowls. Top with lettuce, green onion and coriander; sprinkle with black pepper.

*Dried bamboo shoots are very dark yellow in color and take much longer to cook than either the canned or the fresh variety. Though their initial cooking in 3 quarts (3 L) water seems like an excessive amount of liquid, the volume is necessary to remove some of the yellow color from the shoots.

Variations Cook 8 ounces (250 g) rice vermicelli *(bun)* in a large pot of boiling water about 5 minutes, or until tender. Divide the noodles equally among the bowls before adding the soup, then proceed as directed in the recipe.

Bean-thread noodles *(mien)* may be added to this soup. Soak 2 ounces (60 g) bean-thread noodles in warm water 30 minutes, then cut them into 2-inch (5 cm) lengths. Add the bean-thread noodles to the simmering broth when the duck and bamboo shoots are just cooked and boil gently until the noodles are transparent, about 10 minutes. Proceed as directed in the recipe, but omit the lettuce.

PHO
Beef and Rice Noodle Soup

Pho is a northern Vietnamese specialty, usually eaten for breakfast or as a snack. Most people don't prepare this soup at home because the taste is much better when it is prepared in large quantities. There are many "soup stores" in the cities and towns that specialize in serving *pho*. These stores are as popular as hamburger stands are in the United States. This recipe will serve 12.

3 pounds (1.5 kg) oxtails
10 quarts (10 L) water
6 yellow onions
3 large turnips, peeled and cut into pieces
5 carrots, peeled and cut into pieces
2 tablespoons (30 ml) monosodium glutamate (optional)
1 cup (250 ml) fish sauce *(nuoc mam)*
2 tablespoons (30 ml) chopped ginger root, or 2 teaspoons (10 ml) ground ginger
8 star anise
Fish sauce *(nuoc mam)* to taste
3 tablespoons (45 ml) distilled white vinegar
3 tablespoons (45 ml) water
1 tablespoon (15 ml) sugar
2 pounds (1 kg) dried 1/4-inch-wide (6 mm) flat rice noodles*
1 pound (500 g) bean sprouts
2 pounds (1 kg) lean, tender beef, thinly sliced against the grain
6 green onions, chopped
Several fresh coriander plants, chopped

Ground black pepper
2 limes, each cut into eighths
Fresh red chili pepper slices (optional)

Put the oxtails in a very large soup pot and add the water. Bring to a boil and skim all residue that forms on the surface. Slice 4 of the yellow onions lengthwise and add with the turnips, carrots, monosodium glutamate, fish sauce, ginger and star anise to the pot. Simmer, uncovered, for 8 hours or longer. The longer you can let the broth cook, the better the *pho* will be.

When the broth is almost ready, season to taste with fish sauce. Thinly slice the remaining 2 onions lengthwise. Mix the vinegar, water and sugar, stirring well to dissolve the sugar, and pour over the onions; set aside. Bring a large pot of water to a boil and add the rice noodles. Cook about 8 to 10 minutes, or until tender, drain in a colander and rinse with cold running water. Then rinse the noodles with hot water and divide them equally among 12 bowls. Arrange the bean sprouts on the noodles. Put the beef in a wire strainer and dip the strainer in the simmering broth for a few seconds, then arrange the meat in the bowls. Pour the simmering broth into the bowls and top with green onions and coriander. Sprinkle with black pepper and serve with sliced onions, limes and chili pepper for each person to add according to taste.

*Fresh rice noodles may be substituted for the dried. Place in a colander and immerse in boiling water for only 1 minute before putting them into the bowls.

HU TIU
Pork and Rice Noodle Soup

Another hearty soup that will easily serve 12.

4 pounds (2 kg) pork neck bones
5 medium onions, cut into small pieces
1 cup (250 ml) dried shrimp
10 quarts (10 L) water
2 tablespoons (30 ml) monosodium glutamate
   (optional)
3 tablespoons (45 ml) salt
1/2 cup (125 ml) sugar
8 ounces (250 g) pork shoulder or butt
8 ounces (250 g) medium shrimp, shelled and
   deveined
2 pounds (1 kg) dried 1/4-inch-wide (6 mm)
   flat rice noodles
6 green onions, chopped
Ground black pepper

Combine the neck bones, onions, dried shrimp and water in a very large soup pot. Bring to a boil and skim all residue that forms on the surface. Add the monosodium glutamate and salt and simmer, uncovered, 4 hours. Add the sugar, stirring until it is dissolved.

Put the piece of pork into the broth and simmer until tender, about 15 to 20 minutes. Remove the pork and cut into thin slices. Drop the shrimp into the simmering broth; simmer until done, then remove and cut in half lengthwise. Set the pork and shrimp aside. Bring a large pot of water to a boil and add the rice noodles. Cook about 8 to 10 minutes, or until tender, drain in a colander and rinse with cold running water. Then rinse the noodles with hot water and divide them equally among 12 bowls. Arrange the sliced pork and shrimp over the noodles. Remove the neck bones from the broth and pour the simmering broth into the bowls. Top with green onions and sprinkle with black pepper.

Variations As much pork liver as you wish may also be added. Cook the liver in the broth in the same manner as the pork shoulder and shrimp. Remove, slice thinly and arrange over the noodles with the pork and shrimp.

Fresh or dried wheat noodles *(mi)* may be substituted for the rice noodles. Cook in boiling water until tender (the fresh ones will take much less time) and divide between the bowls as directed for the rice noodles. Fresh rice noodles may also be substituted for the dried ones. Place in a colander and immerse in boiling water for only 1 minute before putting them into the bowls.

MIEN GA
Chicken and Bean-thread Noodle Soup

6 chicken backs
5 tablespoons (75 ml) fish sauce *(nuoc mam)*
4 quarts (4 L) water
2 teaspoons (10 ml) monosodium glutamate
   (optional)
1 tablespoon (15 ml) peanut oil
4 ounces (125 g) boned chicken meat, cut into
   thin strips
1 large onion, sliced lengthwise
Fish sauce *(nuoc mam)*
6 ounces (180 g) bean-thread noodles *(mien)*,
   soaked in warm water 30 minutes, drained
   and cut into 2-inch (5 cm) lengths
Ground black pepper
Chopped green onions and coriander (optional)

Remove all fat from the chicken backs and chop the backs into small pieces. Put the chicken backs and 3 tablespoons (45 ml) of the fish sauce in a large saucepan and cook for a few minutes over medium heat. Add the water, bring to a boil and skim all residue that forms on the surface. Add the monosodium glutamate and simmer, uncovered, 1-1/2 hours or longer.

Heat the oil in a wok or skillet, add the chicken meat, onions and remaining 2 tablespoons (30 ml) fish sauce; stir-fry about 2 minutes. Add to the broth and season to taste with fish sauce. Add the bean-thread noodles and boil gently until the noodles are transparent, about 10 minutes. Just before serving sprinkle with black pepper, green onions and coriander.

Variations Omit the bean-thread noodles. After removing the residue from the broth, add 1 cup (250 ml) well-washed long-grain rice and simmer 1-1/2 hours or longer, stirring occasionally. Proceed as directed in the recipe.

BUN THIT HEO
Pork, Tomatoes and Rice Vermicelli Soup

2 pounds (1 kg) pork neck bones
6 medium tomatoes, sliced lengthwise
2 onions, sliced lengthwise
6 tablespoons (90 ml) fish sauce *(nuoc mam)*
5 quarts (5 L) water
4 ounces (125 g) lean pork shoulder or butt
8 ounces (250 g) rice vermicelli *(bun)*
1 small head lettuce, finely shredded
Fish sauce *(nuoc mam)* to taste
Ground black pepper

Combine the pork bones, tomatoes, onions and fish sauce in a large pot and cook for a few minutes over medium heat. Add the water, bring to a boil, reduce heat and simmer, uncovered, 2 hours or longer.

Cook the piece of pork in the broth until tender, about 10 to 15 minutes. Remove and slice very thin. While the pork is cooking, bring a large pot of water to a boil and cook the rice vermicelli about 5 minutes or until tender. Drain well in a colander and divide among 6 bowls. Arrange the sliced pork on top of the vermicelli and then top with the lettuce. Remove the neck bones and season the broth to taste with fish sauce. Pour the simmering broth into the bowls. Sprinkle with black pepper just before serving.

Seafood

CUA RANG MUOI
Fried Crabs

In Vietnam, Dungeness crabs of only three to four ounces (90 to 125 g) are plentiful, but they are not easily found in the United States. The small blue crab available here can be substituted. Live crabs are preferrable, but if you don't feel you can kill them, buy them already dead or ask the market person to kill them for you.

12 small live crabs
2 teaspoons (10 ml) garlic powder
3 tablespoons (45 ml) salt
2 teaspoons (10 ml) ground black pepper
Peanut oil

To kill the crabs, lay them on their backs on a firm surface, such as a cutting board, and place a Chinese cleaver, blade edge down, on the center of the crab body. With a mallet, firmly strike the top of the knife blade. (If you prefer, you may dip them *very briefly* in boiling water to kill them.) Wash the crabs under cold running water and cut each into quarters with the cleaver. Pound the crab quarters lightly with a heavy knife to crack their shells. Mix the crabs with the garlic powder, salt and black pepper and let stand at least 2 hours. Heat the oil to a depth of about 3 inches (8 cm) in a wok or pan and deep-fry the crabs 5 to 8 minutes, or until cooked. This dish will serve 6.

Variation The crabs may also be stir-fried in 4 to 5 tablespoons (60 to 75 ml) oil in a wok or skillet.

CUA XAO DAM
Sour Crabs

6 small live crabs (see introductory remarks for
   preceding recipe)
4 tablespoons (60 ml) peanut oil
3 tablespoons (45 ml) fish sauce *(nuoc mam)*
2 tablespoons (30 ml) flour
2 tablespoons (30 ml) distilled white vinegar
2 tablespoons (30 ml) sugar
4 tablespoons (60 ml) water
2 onions, sliced lengthwise
Ground black pepper

Follow the directions for preparing the crabs in Cua Rang Muoi (preceding) up to the point where they are seasoned. Heat the oil in a wok or skillet, add the crabs and fish sauce and stir-fry about 2 minutes. Cover and cook over medium heat until crabs are done, about 10 to 15 minutes. Mix together the flour, vinegar, sugar and water, stirring to dissolve the flour and sugar. Add this mixture to the pan and stir until the sauce thickens. Then add the onions and stir-fry 1 to 2 minutes. Transfer to a serving dish and sprinkle with black pepper.

CUA XAO CA CHUA
Crabs and Tomatoes

6 small live crabs (see introductory remarks for
   Cua Rang Muoi, page 122)
6 garlic cloves, crushed
2 tablespoons (30 ml) fish sauce *(nuoc mam)*
1/8 teaspoon (1 ml) ground black pepper
4 tablespoons (60 ml) peanut oil
3 medium tomatoes, sliced lengthwise
Fish sauce *(nuoc mam)* to taste

Follow the directions for preparing the crabs in
Cua Rang Muoi (page 122) up to the point where
they are seasoned. Mix the crab quarters with the
garlic, fish sauce and black pepper. Heat the oil in a
wok or skillet, add the crabs and tomatoes and
stir-fry until cooked, about 10 minutes. Season to
taste with fish sauce.

CUA HAP TRUNG
Steamed Crab Meat

12 ounces (375 g) crab meat, flaked
4 ounces (125 g) ground pork
5 dried mushrooms, soaked in warm water 15
   minutes, drained and finely chopped
1 small onion, finely chopped
3 tablespoons (45 ml) fish sauce *(nuoc mam)*
1/8 teaspoon (1 ml) ground black pepper
2 eggs

Combine the crab meat, pork, mushrooms, onion,
fish sauce and pepper in a bowl and mix thoroughly. Separate one of the eggs and reserve half of its
yolk for use later. Beat the remaining part of the
egg with the second egg and mix into the crab
mixture. Steam the mixture over gently boiling
water about 30 to 40 minutes, or until pork is
cooked. Beat the reserved half egg yolk with chopsticks or a fork and pour over the steamed crab
mixture. Steam 5 minutes longer and serve.

BAP CAI NHOI TOM THIT
Shrimp and Pork with Cabbage

8 ounces (250 g) ground pork
8 ounces (250 g) medium shrimp, shelled and deveined
2 ounces (60 g) bean-thread noodles, soaked in
   warm water 30 minutes, drained and cut into
   1-inch (3 cm) lengths
6 dried mushrooms or wood fungus, soaked in
   warm water 30 minutes, drained and cut into
   matchstick strips
2 small onions, finely chopped
4 tablespoons (60 ml) fish sauce *(nuoc mam)*
1/8 teaspoon (1 ml) ground black pepper
24 large cabbage leaves (about 1 small head)

Combine the pork, shrimp, noodles, mushrooms or
wood fungus, onions, fish sauce and black pepper
and mix well; set aside. Bring a large pot of water
to a boil and dip the cabbage leaves into the water
for 1 to 2 minutes, or until they are soft and
pliable. Form the pork-shrimp mixture into 24
balls and wrap each ball in a cabbage leaf, securing
the leaf in place with a piece of thread or a wooden
pick. Steam the cabbage rolls above gently boiling
water 30 minutes.

TOM VIEN
Shrimp Balls

These shrimp balls make an excellent hors d'oeuvre or can be served with rice as part of a meal. In Vietnam, the shrimp paste is often formed around sugar cane and charcoal broiled or the balls are served in soup.

1 teaspoon (5 ml) salt
1 pound (500 g) medium shrimp, shelled and deveined
1 ounce (30 g) pork fat, finely chopped
5 garlic cloves, finely chopped
3 shallots, finely chopped
1/8 teaspoon (1 ml) ground black pepper
2 teaspoons (10 ml) sugar
1 tablespoon (15 ml) fish sauce *(nuoc mam)*
1 tablespoon (15 ml) cornstarch
1 egg white, lightly beaten
Peanut oil for deep-frying
Fish sauce *(nuoc mam)* or soy sauce

Sprinkle the salt over the shrimp and mix well. Let stand 30 minutes, then wash off the salt thoroughly and drain well. Finely chop the shrimp and mix with the pork fat, garlic and shallots. Either pound in a mortar until a paste is formed or whirl in a blender container, adding a little oil or some of the fish sauce if the motor of the blender begins to labor. Mix the pepper, sugar, fish sauce, cornstarch and egg white into the shrimp paste and form the mixture into balls 1 inch (3 cm) in diameter. Heat the oil to a depth of about 1 inch (3 cm) in a wok or skillet to about 375°F (190°C) and deep-fry the shrimp balls until golden, about 2 to 3 minutes. Serve with fish sauce or soy sauce for dipping.

TOM XAO RAU
Shrimp with Vegetables

8 ounces (250 g) medium shrimp, shelled and deveined
1 tablespoon (15 ml) fish sauce *(nuoc mam)*
1/8 teaspoon (1 ml) ground black pepper
1 teaspoon (5 ml) chopped onion
1 cucumber
3 tablespoons (45 ml) peanut oil
8 ounces (250 g) Chinese cabbage *(bok choy)*
2 or 3 slices ginger root
Fish sauce *(nuoc mam)* to taste
Chopped fresh coriander
Ground black pepper

Combine the shrimp, fish sauce, black pepper and onion and set aside. Cut the cucumber crosswise into thirds. Cut the thirds in half lengthwise and scoop out the seeds, then cut lengthwise into strips 1/8 inch (3 mm) wide. Heat 2 tablespoons (30 ml) of the oil in a wok or skillet, add the shrimp and stir-fry about 3 minutes, or until they turn pink and are cooked. Remove the shrimp with a slotted utensil and set aside. Add the remaining 1 tablespoon (15 ml) oil to the pan and heat until very hot. Add the cucumber and stir-fry 2 minutes. Add the Chinese cabbage and ginger root and stir-fry about 1 minute or until vegetables are cooked. Return the shrimp to the pan and season to taste with fish sauce. Transfer to a serving dish and sprinkle with coriander and black pepper.

CA XAO CHUA
Fish and Tomatoes

1 pound (500 g) fresh fish fillets, such as bass,
   perch, carp or bluefish
3 tablespoons (45 ml) peanut oil
3 tablespoons (45 ml) fish sauce *(nuoc mam)*
1/8 teaspoon (1 ml) ground black pepper
3 shallots, thinly sliced
4 tomatoes, chopped
1/2 cup (125 ml) water
1 tablespoon (15 ml) flour, dissolved in
   3 tablespoons water
Fish sauce *(nuoc mam)* to taste
2 teaspoons (10 ml) distilled white vinegar
Ground black pepper

Divide the fish fillets so that you have 4 equal pieces. Heat 1 tablespoon (15 ml) of the oil in a wok or skillet, add the fish and lightly brown on both sides. Remove the fish with a slotted utensil and sprinkle with 1 tablespoon (15 ml) of the fish sauce and the black pepper, turning to coat well; set aside. Heat the remaining 2 tablespoons oil in the same pan and brown the shallots. Add the tomatoes, the remaining 2 tablespoons (30 ml) fish sauce and the water. Simmer over medium heat until the tomatoes are soft. Return the fish to the pan and stir in the flour mixture. Continue stirring until the sauce thickens, then season to taste with fish sauce. Stir in the vinegar and transfer to a serving dish. Sprinkle with black pepper.

MUC XAO RAU
Fresh Squid and Vegetables

8 ounces (250 g) squid
2 tablespoons (30 ml) fish sauce (nuoc mam)
1/8 teaspoon (1 ml) ground black pepper
4 tablespoons (60 ml) peanut oil
3 shallots, thinly sliced
4 carrots, peeled and thinly sliced on the diagonal
1/4 cup (50 ml) water
4 onions, sliced lengthwise
1 cup (250 ml) snow peas
2 slices ginger root
Fish sauce (nuoc mam) to taste
1 tablespoon (15 ml) chopped fresh coriander
Ground black pepper

Rinse the squid in cold water. Separate the tentacles from the tail section by gently pulling apart, being careful not to break the ink sac. Discard the ink sac and the transparent, sword-shaped cartilage in the tail section. Cut off the tentacles above the eye section and discard the eye section. Force out the small round cartilege at the base of the tentacles with your fingertips, discard the cartilege, and set the tentacles aside. Rinse the tail section and pull off the blotchy membrane. Slice the tail section in 1-inch-long (3 cm) pieces. Mix the squid bodies and tentacles with 1 tablespoon (15 ml) of the fish sauce and the pepper and let stand 30 minutes.

Heat 2 tablespoons (30 ml) of the peanut oil in a wok or skillet and brown the shallots. Add the squid and stir-fry about 2 minutes. Do not overcook or the squid will be tough. Remove the squid with a slotted utensil; leave the juices in the pan. Add the remaining 2 tablespoons (30 ml) oil to the pan and heat until very hot. Add the carrots and stir-fry 1 minute. Add the water and continue to stir-fry until the carrots are almost cooked. Then add the onions, snow peas, remaining 1 tablespoon (15 ml) fish sauce and ginger and stir-fry 1 minute. Return the squid to the pan and season to taste with fish sauce. Transfer to a serving dish and sprinkle with coriander and black pepper.

CA HAP
Steamed Trout

One 1-pound (500 g) trout
1/2 cup (125 ml) thinly sliced pork shoulder with
   a little fat
1 tablespoon (15 ml) finely shredded ginger root
1 teaspoon (5 ml) sugar
4 shallots, thinly sliced
1/8 teaspoon (1 ml) ground black pepper
4 tablespoons (60 ml) fish sauce (nuoc mam)
4 dried mushrooms, soaked in warm water 15
   minutes, drained and cut into matchstick
1 tablespoon (15 ml) chopped fresh coriander
   (optional)
Ground black pepper

You may leave the fish whole or cut it into 4 pieces. Make a few shallow diagonal slashes on both sides of the fish and place in a shallow bowl that can be used for steaming. Mix together the pork, ginger, sugar, shallots, black pepper and fish sauce and coat the fish with the mixture. Let stand 30 minutes. Arrange the mushrooms on top of the fish and steam above gently boiling water 30 to 40 minutes, or until fish flakes easily. Just before serving, sprinkle with coriander and black pepper.

Poultry

GA XAO DUA
Chicken and Pineapple

2 tablespoons (30 ml) peanut oil
8 ounces (250 g) chicken meat, cut into 1-inch
 (3 cm) pieces
2 tablespoons (30 ml) fish sauce *(nuoc mam)*
1 small pineapple, cleaned and cut into 1/2-inch
 (1.5 cm) pieces
1 to 2 celery stalks, cut on the diagonal into 1-inch
 (3 cm) pieces
1 tablespoon (15 ml) cornstarch, dissolved in
 3 tablespoons (45 ml) water
Fish sauce *(nuoc mam)* or ground black pepper
 to taste

Heat the oil in a wok or skillet, add the chicken and 1 tablespoon (15 ml) of the fish sauce and stir-fry 2 minutes. Add the pineapple, celery and remaining 1 tablespoon (15 ml) fish sauce and stir-fry 1 minute. Stir in the cornstarch mixture and heat briefly until juices thicken. Season to taste with fish sauce. Transfer to a serving dish and sprinkle with black pepper.

GA XAO NAM ROM
Chicken and Mushrooms

8 ounces (250 g) chicken meat, cut into 1-inch
 (3 cm) pieces
2 tablespoons (30 ml) fish sauce *(nuoc mam)*
1/8 teaspoon (1 ml) monosodium glutamate
 (optional)
2 tablespoons (30 ml) peanut oil
8 ounces (250 g) fresh mushrooms, sliced
1 teaspoon (5 ml) finely chopped ginger root
Fish sauce *(nuoc mam)* and ground black pepper
 to taste

Combine the chicken, 1 tablespoon (15 ml) of the fish sauce and the monosodium glutamate and let stand 30 minutes. Heat the oil in a wok or skillet, add the chicken and stir-fry 2 minutes. Add the mushrooms, the remaining 1 tablespoon (15 ml) fish sauce and the ginger and stir-fry until chicken and mushrooms are cooked. Season to taste with fish sauce. Transfer to a serving dish and sprinkle with black pepper.

Variation Substitute 8 ounces (250 g) snow peas for the mushrooms. Proceed as directed in the recipe.

GA CHUA NGOT
Sweet and Sour Chicken

1/4 cup (60 ml) sugar
1/4 cup (60 ml) distilled white vinegar
1/4 cup (60 ml) water
8 chicken wings
3 tablespoons (45 ml) fish sauce *(nuoc mam)*
2 large onions, sliced lengthwise

Combine the sugar, vinegar and water and stir well to dissolve the sugar; set aside. The chicken wings may be left whole or cut into 3 pieces at the joints. Heat the chicken wings and fish sauce in a wok or skillet and stir-fry until wings are almost cooked. Add the sugar-vinegar mixture and stir-fry until the sauce is almost completely absorbed into the chicken. Add the onions and stir-fry 2 to 3 minutes.

Variations Substitute chicken thighs or drumsticks, cut into 1-1/2-inch (4 cm) pieces on the bone, for the wings.

CANH GA CHIEN BO
Fried Chicken Wings

The butter in this recipe, though not traditional, gives an excellent flavor to the chicken. Its use can be attributed to the influence of French cooking in Vietnam.

8 chicken wings
1 teaspoon (5 ml) salt
2 teaspoons (10 ml) thin soy sauce
1 teaspoon (5 ml) garlic powder
1 teaspoon (5 ml) ground black pepper
Peanut oil for deep-frying
2 tablespoons (30 ml) butter

The chicken wings may be left whole or cut into 3 pieces at the joints. Combine the chicken wings, salt, soy sauce, garlic powder and black pepper and let stand about 2 hours. Heat the oil to a depth of 2 inches (5 cm) in a wok or pan until very hot. Add the butter and let it melt, then deep-fry the chicken wings until browned and crispy.

Variations Chicken thighs or drumsticks may be substituted for the wings.

GA XAO XA OT
Chicken with Lemon Grass and Chili

8 ounces (250 g) boned chicken meat, cut into
    1/2-inch (1.5 cm) pieces
1 tablespoon (15 ml) fish sauce *(nuoc mam)*
1/2 teaspoon (3 ml) curry powder
1 tablespoon (15 ml) chopped fresh lemon grass
    (xa), or
    2 teaspoons (10 ml) chopped or crushed dried
    lemon grass
1/8 teaspoon (1 ml) finely chopped fresh red chili
    pepper, or more to taste
2 tablespoons (30 ml) peanut oil
Fish sauce *(nuoc mam)* to taste

Combine the chicken, fish sauce, curry powder, lemon grass and chili pepper. Heat the oil in a wok or skillet, add the chicken and stir-fry until cooked. Season to taste with fish sauce.

GA XAO HANH NHAN
Chicken and Almonds

8 ounces (250 g) boned chicken meat, cut into
   1/2-inch (1.5 cm) pieces
2 tablespoons (30 ml) fish sauce *(nuoc mam)*
1/8 teaspoon (1 ml) ground black pepper
4 tablespoons (60 ml) peanut oil
3 shallots, thinly sliced
4 carrots, thinly sliced
1/2 cup (125 ml) water
6 ounces (180 g) roasted almonds
1 tablespoon (15 ml) cornstarch, dissolved in
   3 tablespoons (45 ml) water
1 cup (250 ml) snow peas
Fish sauce *(nuoc mam)* and ground black pepper
   to taste

Combine the chicken, 1 tablespoon (15 ml) of the fish sauce and the black pepper. Heat 2 tablespoons (30 ml) of the oil in a wok or skillet and brown the shallots. Add the chicken and stir-fry until tender. Remove from the pan with a slotted utensil and set aside. Add the remaining 2 tablespoons (30 ml) oil to the pan and heat until hot. Add the carrots and stir-fry 2 minutes. Add the water and cook until carrots are almost tender. Add the almonds, the remaining 1 tablespoon (15 ml) fish sauce and the cornstarch mixture and heat briefly to thicken the juices. Return the chicken to the pan, add the snow peas and stir-fry 1 minute. Season to taste with fish sauce and transfer to a serving platter. Sprinkle with black pepper.

Note Blanched almonds may be used in place of the roasted ones. Brown them in a dry pan over *very low* heat before adding to the wok.

GA NAU NAM
Stewed Chicken and Mushrooms

3 tablespoons (45 ml) peanut oil
12 to 16 chicken thighs
5 shallots, sliced
1 tablespoon (15 ml) flour
2 tablespoons (30 ml) fish sauce *(nuoc mam)*
1 teaspoon (5 ml) monosodium glutamate
   (optional)
1/4 teaspoon (1 to 2 ml) ground black pepper
1 quart (1 L) chicken stock or water
6 ounces (180 g) fresh or canned button
   mushrooms
1 tablespoon (15 ml) butter
1 tablespoon (15 ml) tomato paste
Fish sauce *(nuoc mam)* to taste

Heat the oil in a wok or heavy saucepan and fry the chicken thighs until lightly golden. Remove from pan with a slotted utensil and set aside. Add the shallots to the pan and fry until browned. Then add the flour and fry, stirring constantly, until golden. Return the chicken to the pan and add the fish sauce, monosodium glutamate, black pepper and chicken stock or water. Bring to a boil, reduce heat and simmer, covered, until chicken is tender, about 35 to 45 minutes. Add the mushrooms, butter and tomato paste and simmer a few minutes. Season to taste with fish sauce. This dish will serve 6 persons.

GA NAU DAU
Stewed Chicken and Peas

3 tablespoons (45 ml) peanut oil
12 to 16 chicken thighs
2 medium onions, chopped
2 garlic cloves, crushed
2 tablespoons (30 ml) fish sauce *(nuoc mam)*
1/4 teaspoon (1 to 2 ml) ground black pepper
1 teaspoon (5 ml) monosodium glutamate
   (optional)
1 quart (1 L) chicken stock or water
3/4 cup (175 ml) shelled green peas
Fish sauce *(nuoc mam)* and ground black pepper
   to taste

Heat the oil in a wok or heavy saucepan and fry the chicken until lightly golden. Add the onions, garlic, fish sauce, pepper, monosodium glutamate and stock or water. Bring to a boil, reduce heat, cover and simmer until chicken is tender, about 40 to 45 minutes. Add the peas and simmer a few minutes. Season to taste with fish sauce and transfer to a serving dish. Sprinkle with black pepper.

GA NUONG CHAO
Baked Spiced Chicken

8 pieces canned cured bean curd, with or without
   chili pepper
2 teaspoons (10 ml) garlic powder
1 tablespoon (15 ml) finely chopped onion
2 teaspoons (10 ml) salt
1 teaspoon (5 ml) ground black pepper
1 whole chicken, about 3 pounds (1.5 kg)
2 tablespoons (30 ml) tapioca flour
2 tablespoons (30 ml) distilled white vinegar
1 tablespoon (15 ml) water
2 teaspoons (10 ml) honey
2 teaspoons (10 ml) Oriental-style sesame oil
Lettuce leaves or watercress sprigs

In a bowl, beat the bean curd with chopsticks or a fork until well broken up. Add the garlic, onion, salt and pepper and mix well. Rub this mixture over the chicken inside and out and let stand 1 hour. Mix together the tapioca flour, vinegar, water and honey, stirring well to dissolve the tapioca flour. Wipe the chicken dry with paper toweling and brush the tapioca flour mixture over the chicken skin. Hang chicken in a drafty, shady area and let it dry about 2 hours.

   Put the chicken in a roasting pan breast side up and roast in a preheated 300°F (150°C) oven about 1-1/2 hours, or until juices run clear when joint is pierced with a fork. Just before chicken is done, brush sesame oil over the skin several times. To serve, cut into bite-size pieces on the bone and place on platter lined with lettuce leaves or watercress sprigs.

GA TIM
Stuffed Chicken

1 whole chicken, about 3 pounds (1.5 kg)
1 quart (1 L) chicken stock or water
1 teaspoon (5 ml) monosodium glutamate
   (optional)
Fish sauce *(nuoc mam)* to taste

Stuffing
1/4 cup (60 ml) lotus seeds or roasted almonds
4 ounces (125 g) ground pork
10 medium dried mushrooms, soaked in warm
   water to soften, drained and chopped
5 shallots, finely chopped
3 tablespoons (45 ml) fish sauce *(nuoc mam)*
1/2 teaspoon (2 to 3 ml) ground black pepper

To make the stuffing, boil the lotus seeds or almonds in water to cover 15 minutes; drain, and if
using almonds, skin them. Chop the lotus seeds or
almonds and combine with the pork, mushrooms,
shallots, fish sauce and black pepper. Stuff this
mixture into the chicken cavity and truss closed.
Place the chicken in a large deep bowl and steam
over gently boiling water about 40 minutes, or
until almost cooked. Combine the chicken stock or
water, monosodium glutamate and fish sauce in a
large pot and set the chicken in it. Bring to a gentle
boil, reduce heat, cover and simmer about 10 to 15
minutes. During this "second cooking," the chick-
en will absorb flavor from the stock. Remove from
the stock and cut into serving pieces. This dish will
serve 6 persons.

VIT NUONG
Roast Duck

1/2 cup (125 ml) thin soy sauce
1 tablespoon (15 ml) finely chopped or grated
   ginger root
1 teaspoon (5 ml) sugar
1 teaspoon (5 ml) garlic powder
4 garlic cloves, crushed
One 4-pound (2 kg) duck
Ginger sauce (following recipe)

Combine the soy sauce, ginger, sugar, garlic powder
and garlic cloves. Rub the mixture on the duck
inside and out and let stand 2 hours. Roast on a
rack, breast side up, in a preheated 300°F (150°C)
oven 1-1/2 hours, or until juices run clear when
joint is pierced with a fork. Brush occasionally
with the juices that collect in the pan. Cut into
bite-size pieces on the bone to serve. Serve with
ginger sauce for dipping.

Ginger sauce Combine 2 tablespoons (30 ml)
grated ginger root, 5 tablespoons (75 ml) thin soy
sauce, 1 tablespoon (15 ml) sugar, 2 teaspoons (10
ml) distilled white vinegar and 1 tablespoon
(15 ml) water and mix well.

Note This duck is excellent served with steamed
glutinous rice (page 108, with chicken meat
omitted).

Beef & Pork

BO XAO BONG CAI
Beef with Cauliflower

8 ounces (250 g) beef flank steak or other tender
   cut, cut against the grain into slices 1-1/2 by
   1 by 1/8 inch (4 cm by 3 cm by 3 mm)
2 tablespoons (30 ml) fish sauce *(nuoc mam)*
1/8 teaspoon (1 ml) garlic powder
1/8 teaspoon (1 ml) ground black pepper
3 tablespoons (45 ml) peanut oil
1 garlic clove, crushed
1 medium cauliflower, broken into flowerets
1 cup (250 ml) beef stock or water
Fish sauce *(nuoc mam)* and ground black pepper
   to taste

Combine the beef, 1 tablespoon (15 ml) of the fish sauce, the garlic powder and black pepper and let stand 30 minutes. Heat 2 tablespoons (30 ml) of the oil in a wok or skillet and brown the garlic clove. Discard the garlic, add the beef to the pan and stir-fry until browned. Remove with a slotted utensil and set aside; leave the juices in the pan. Add the remaining 1 tablespoon (15 ml) oil to the pan juices and heat until very hot. Add the cauliflower, beef stock or water and the remaining 1 tablespoon (15 ml) fish sauce. Stir-fry until cauliflower is just tender. Return the beef to the pan and mix thoroughly. Season to taste with fish sauce and sprinkle with black pepper.

Note If a thicker sauce is desired, dissolve 1 tablespoon (15 ml) tapioca flour in 3 tablespoons (45 ml) beef stock or water and stir into pan at end of cooking. Heat briefly until juices thicken.

Variation Substitute 8 ounces (250 g) green beans, cut on the diagonal into 2-inch (5 cm) lengths, for the cauliflower. Proceed as directed in the recipe.

BO XAO GIA
Beef with Bean Sprouts

12 ounces (375 g) beef flank steak or other tender
   cut, cut against the grain into slices 1-1/2 by 1
   by 1/8 inch (4 cm by 3 cm by 3 mm)
3 tablespoons (45 ml) fish sauce *(nuoc mam)*
1/8 teaspoon (1 ml) garlic powder
1/8 teaspoon (1 ml) ground black pepper
1 small onion, sliced lengthwise
4 tablespoons (60 ml) peanut oil
2 garlic cloves, crushed
2 pounds (1 kg) bean sprouts
Fish sauce *(nuoc mam)* and ground black pepper to
   taste

Combine the beef, 1 tablespoon (15 ml) of the fish
sauce, garlic powder, black pepper and onion and
let stand 30 minutes. Heat 2 tablespoons (30 ml)
of the oil in a wok or skillet and brown the garlic
cloves. Discard the garlic, add the beef to the pan
and stir-fry until browned. Remove with a slotted
utensil and set aside; leave the juices in the pan.
Add the remaining 2 tablespoons (30 ml) oil to the
pan juices and heat until very hot. Add the bean
sprouts and remaining 2 tablespoons (30 ml) fish
sauce and stir-fry until the bean sprouts begin to
become translucent. (The bean sprouts should remain crunchy.) Return the beef to the pan and mix
thoroughly. Season to taste with fish sauce and
sprinkle with black pepper.

BO XAO CA CHUA
Beef with Tomatoes

12 ounces (375 g) beef flank steak or other tender
   cut, cut against the grain into slices 1-1/2 by 1
   by 1/8 inch (4 cm by 3 cm by 3 mm)
1/8 teaspoon (1 ml) garlic powder
1/8 teaspoon (1 ml) ground black pepper
2 tablespoons (30 ml) fish sauce *(nuoc mam)*
3 tablespoons (45 ml) peanut oil
1 garlic clove, crushed
3 small or 2 large tomatoes, sliced lengthwise
1/2 cup (125 ml) water
Fish sauce *(nuoc mam)* to taste
1 tablespoon (15 ml) chopped green onion
Ground black pepper
1 tablespoon (15 ml) chopped fresh coriander
Shredded lettuce

Combine the beef, garlic powder, black pepper and
1 tablespoon (15 ml) of the fish sauce and let stand
30 minutes. Heat 2 tablespoons (30 ml) of the oil
in a wok or skillet and brown the garlic clove.
Discard the garlic, add the beef to the pan and
stir-fry until browned. Remove with a slotted utensil and set aside; leave the juices in the pan. Add
the remaining 1 tablespoon (15 ml) oil to the pan
juices and heat until very hot. Add the tomatoes,
the remaining 1 tablespoon (15 ml) fish sauce and
the water. Stir-fry until tomatoes are just soft.
Return the beef to the pan and mix thoroughly.
Season to taste with fish sauce and mix in green
onions. Transfer to a serving dish and sprinkle with
black pepper and coriander. Serve lettuce in a
separate dish as a salad.

BO XAO KHOAI TAY
Beef with Fried Potatoes

1 pound (500 g) beef flank steak or other tender
    cut, cut against the grain into slices 1-1/2 by 1
    by 1/8 inch (4 cm by 3 cm by 3 mm)
2 tablespoons (30 ml) fish sauce *(nuoc mam)*
1/4 teaspoon (1 to 2 ml) garlic powder
1/4 teaspoon (1 to 2 ml) ground black pepper
6 medium potatoes, peeled
1 teaspoon (5 ml) salt
Peanut or vegetable oil
2 garlic cloves, crushed
1 medium onion, sliced lengthwise about 1/8
    inch (3 mm) thick
Ground black pepper to taste

Combine the beef, fish sauce, garlic powder and black pepper and let stand 30 minutes. Cut the potatoes crosswise into slices about three times thicker than potato chips, then sprinkle the salt over them. Heat the oil to a depth of 3 inches (8 cm) in a wok or pot until very hot (about 375°F or 190°C) and deep-fry the potatoes until golden brown. Remove with a slotted utensil and drain on paper toweling. Transfer to a warmed platter.

    Heat 2 tablespoons (30 ml) oil in a wok or skillet and brown the garlic cloves. Discard the garlic, add the beef and onion and stir-fry until the beef is browned. Pour the beef over the potatoes and sprinkle with black pepper to taste.

Note If a thicker sauce is desired, dissolve 1 tablespoon (15 ml) tapioca flour in 3 tablespoons (45 ml) water and stir into the pan at the end of cooking. Heat briefly until juices thicken.

BO CHIEN
Fried Beef

1 pound (500 g) beef flank steak or other tender
    cut, cut against the grain into slices 1-1/2 by
    1/2 by 1/2 inch (4 by 1.5 by 1.5 cm)
2 tablespoons (30 ml) fish sauce *(nuoc mam)*
1 tablespoon (15 ml) plus 2 teaspoons (10 ml)
    sugar
1/4 teaspoon (1 to 2 ml) garlic powder
1/4 teaspoon (1 to 2 ml) ground black pepper
1/2 teaspoon (2 ml) monosodium glutamate
    (optional)
2 medium onions, sliced crosswise
3 tablespoons (45 ml) distilled white vinegar
3 tablespoons (45 ml) water
Romaine lettuce leaves
3 tablespoons (45 ml) peanut oil
2 garlic cloves, crushed
Ground black pepper to taste

Combine the beef, fish sauce, 2 teaspoons (10 ml) of the sugar, the garlic powder, black pepper and monosodium glutamate and let stand 30 minutes. Combine the onions, vinegar, water and remaining 1 tablespoon (15 ml) sugar and let stand a few minutes to allow flavors to blend.

    Arrange the lettuce leaves on a large platter and scatter the onion rings on top of them. Heat the oil in a wok or skillet and brown the garlic cloves. Discard the garlic, add the beef and stir-fry until browned. Pour meat over onion rings and lettuce leaves and sprinkle with black pepper to taste.

BO XAO HANH TAY
Beef with Onions

12 ounces (375 g) beef flank steak or other tender
   cut, cut against the grain into slices 1-1/2 by 1
   by 1/8 inch (4 cm by 3 cm by 3 mm)
2 tablespoons (30 ml) fish sauce *(nuoc mam)*
1/8 teaspoon (1 ml) garlic powder
1/8 teaspoon (1 ml) ground black pepper
2 tablespoons (30 ml) peanut oil
2 garlic cloves, crushed
4 large onions, sliced lengthwise about 1/8 inch
   (3 mm) thick
Fish sauce *(nuoc mam)* and ground black pepper
   to taste

Combine the beef, 1 tablespoon (15 ml) of the fish
sauce, the garlic powder and black pepper; let stand
30 minutes. Heat the oil in a wok or skillet and
brown the garlic cloves. Discard the garlic, add the
beef, onions and remaining 1 tablespoon (15 ml)
fish sauce to the pan and stir-fry until the beef is
browned. Season to taste with fish sauce. Transfer
to a serving dish and sprinkle with black pepper.

BO NHUNG DAM
Beef Fondue

Carrots and turnips
2 carrots
2 turnips
3 tablespoons (45 ml) distilled white vinegar
3 tablespoons (45 ml) water
1 tablespoon (15 ml) sugar

Nuoc mam sauce
6 tablespoons (90 ml) fish sauce *(nuoc mam)*
2 tablespoons (30 ml) water
1 tablespoon (15 ml) sugar
1 teaspoon (5 ml) fresh lemon juice
1/2 teaspoon (3 ml) finely chopped garlic
Fresh red chili pepper slices (optional)

1-3/4 cups (400 ml) distilled white vinegar
1-3/4 cups (400 ml) water
5 tablespoons (75 ml) sugar
1 cup (250 ml) beef stock
2 teaspoons (10 ml) chopped or crushed dried
   lemon grass *(xa)*
2 teaspoons (10 ml) chopped green onion
1 pound (500 g) tender beef steak, thinly sliced
1 small head iceberg lettuce, cut into pieces 1-1/2
   by 1 inch (4 by 3 cm)

To prepare the carrots and turnips, peel them and
cut into thin rounds or thin rectangular slices 1-1/2
inches (4 cm) long by 1 inch (3 cm) wide. Combine
the vinegar, water and sugar and stir until sugar is
dissolved. Pour over the carrot and turnip slices
and set aside. To make the *nuoc mam* sauce, combine all the ingredients and mix well; set aside.

Combine the vinegar, water, sugar, beef stock,
lemon grass and green onion in a fondue pot or any
pot that can be placed over a hot plate or brazier.
Bring to a boil, stirring well to dissolve the sugar.
Provide each diner with a pair of chopsticks for
holding the beef in the boiling mixture until
cooked to desired doneness. Serve with the carrots
and turnips, *nuoc mam* sauce and lettuce.

BO NUONG
Charcoal-broiled Beef

Traditionally, a small charcoal grill is placed in the center of the table and each diner cooks his own beef.

1 pound (500 g) beef flank steak or other tender
    cut, cut against the grain into slices 1-1/2 by 1
    by 1/16 inch (4 cm by 3 cm by 1.5 mm)
2 tablespoons (30 ml) finely chopped green onion
2 tablespoons (30 ml) fish sauce *(nuoc mam)*
2 teaspoons (10 ml) sugar
1 teaspoon (5 ml) monosodium glutamate
    (optional)
2 tablespoons (30 ml) sesame seeds
1 tablespoon (15 ml) chopped or crushed dried
    lemon grass *(xa)*
2 tablespoons (30 ml) lard or peanut oil
Carrots and turnips (page 138)
1 small head iceberg lettuce, cut into pieces 1-1/2
    by 1 inch (4 by 3 cm)
Nuoc mam sauce (page 138)

Combine the beef, onions, fish sauce, sugar, monosodium glutamate, sesame seeds and lemon grass. Heat the lard or oil in a small pan until hot and pour it over the meat mixture. Mix briefly and refrigerate for a few hours. Prepare the carrots and turnips, lettuce and *nuoc mam* sauce.

    Arrange the meat on a grill over a charcoal fire. Cook until browned, turning once. Arrange the beef on a platter. Serve carrots and turnips, lettuce and *nuoc mam* sauce on the side.

Note The beef may also be arranged on a baking sheet and cooked in a 300°F (150°C) oven 20 to 25 minutes.

BO XAO CA CHUA CAN
Beef with Tomatoes and Celery

8 ounces (250 g) beef flank steak or other tender
    cut, cut against the grain into slices 1-1/2 by 1
    by 1/8 inch (4 cm by 3 cm by 3 mm)
2 tablespoons (30 ml) fish sauce *(nuoc mam)*
1/8 teaspoon (1 ml) garlic powder
1/8 teaspoon (1 ml) ground black pepper
3 tablespoons (45 ml) peanut oil
1 garlic clove, crushed
4 medium ripe tomatoes, sliced lengthwise about
    1/2 inch (1.5 cm) thick
2 celery stalks, cut on the diagonal into 1/2-inch
    (1.5 cm) lengths
Fish sauce *(nuoc mam)* and ground black pepper
    to taste

Combine the beef, fish sauce, garlic powder and black pepper and let stand 30 minutes. Heat 2 tablespoons (30 ml) of the oil in a wok or skillet and brown the garlic clove. Discard the garlic, add the beef and stir-fry until browned. Remove with a slotted utensil and set aside; leave the juices in the pan. Add the remaining 1 tablespoon (15 ml) oil to the pan juices and heat until very hot. Add the tomatoes and celery and stir-fry until the vegetables are cooked but not too soft. Return the beef to the pan and mix thoroughly. Season to taste with fish sauce and sprinkle with black pepper.

BO XAO RAU
Beef with Vegetables

8 ounces (250 g) beef flank steak or other tender
    cut, cut against the grain into slices 1-1/2 by 1
    by 1/8 inch (4 cm by 3 cm by 3 mm)
3 tablespoons (45 ml) fish sauce *(nuoc mam)*
1/8 teaspoon (1 ml) garlic powder
1/8 teaspoon (1 ml) ground black pepper
4 tablespoons (60 ml) peanut oil
2 garlic cloves, crushed
3 cups (750 ml) shredded cabbage
2 carrots, cut into thin rectangular slices 1-1/2
    inches (4 cm) long by 1 inch (3 cm) wide
1-1/2 cups (375 ml) water
2 medium onions, sliced lengthwise
1 celery stalk, cut on the diagonal into 1-1/2-
    inch (4 cm) lengths 1/4 inch (6 mm) wide
Fish sauce *(nuoc mam)* to taste
1 tablespoon (15 ml) tapioca flour, dissolved in
    3 tablespoons (45 ml) water
Ground black pepper to taste

Combine the beef, 1 tablespoon (15 ml) of the fish
sauce, the garlic powder and black pepper and let
stand 30 minutes. Heat 2 tablespoons (30 ml) of
the oil in a wok or skillet and brown the garlic
cloves. Discard the garlic, add the beef to the pan
and stir-fry until browned. Remove with a slotted
utensil and set aside; leave the juices in the pan.
Add the remaining 2 tablespoons (30 ml) oil to the
pan juices and heat until very hot. Add the cabbage, carrots, 1 tablespoon (15 ml) of the fish
sauce and the water. Cook, stirring, until vegetables
are almost cooked. Then add onions, celery and
the remaining 1 tablespoon (15 ml) fish sauce and

continue to cook until vegetables are just tender.
Return the beef to the pan and mix thoroughly.
Season with fish sauce to taste. Add the tapioca
flour mixture to the pan and heat briefly until
juices thicken. Transfer to a serving dish and sprinkle with black pepper.

BO KHO
Beef Stew

1 pound (500 g) beef stew meat, cut into 1-1/2-
    inch (4 cm) cubes
2 slices ginger root, crushed with the flat side of
    a cleaver and peeled, or
    1/2 teaspoon (2 to 3 ml) ground ginger
3 tablespoons (45 ml) fish sauce *(nuoc mam)*
2 teaspoons (10 ml) curry powder
1 quart (1 L) water
3 star anise
3 carrots, peeled and cut into 1/2-inch (1.5 cm)
    lengths
Fish sauce *(nuoc mam)* to taste
Fresh chili pepper slices (optional)
Ground black pepper to taste

Combine the beef, ginger root, fish sauce and curry
powder and let stand 1 hour. Combine the beef,
water, star anise and carrots in a wok or saucepan
and bring to a boil. Reduce heat, cover and simmer
until beef is tender, about 1 hour. Season to taste
with fish sauce and add chili pepper slices, if desired. Transfer to a serving dish and sprinkle with
black pepper.

CA-RI BO
Curry Beef

This dish reflects the influence of Indian food on the cuisine of Vietnam.

1 pound (500 g) beef stew meat, cut into 1-1/2-
   inch (4 cm) cubes
3 garlic cloves, crushed
3 shallots, crushed
1/2 teaspoon (2 to 3 ml) ground black pepper
1 tablespoon (15 ml) salt
4 tablespoons (60 ml) peanut or vegetable oil
1 tablespoon (15 ml) curry powder or to taste
6 cups (1.5 L) water
4 medium potatoes, peeled and cut into sixths

Combine the beef, garlic, shallots, black pepper and salt; let stand 1 hour. Heat 1 tablespoon (15 ml) of the oil in a wok or heavy pot and fry beef until browned. Add the curry powder and water, bring to a boil, reduce heat, cover and simmer until the beef is tender, about 1 hour. While the beef is cooking, heat the remaining 3 tablespoons (45 ml) oil in a wok or skillet and fry the potatoes until golden brown and tender. Add the potatoes to the beef and simmer, uncovered, until sauce thickens slightly. Taste and adjust seasoning with salt.

Variation Substitute 1-1/2 pounds (750 g) chicken breasts or thighs, cut into 1-1/2-inch (4 cm) pieces on the bone, for the beef. Proceed as directed, but cook only 25 to 30 minutes, or until tender, before adding potatoes.

CAT HEO XAO RAU
Pork Kidney and Vegetables

1 pound (500 g) pork kidneys
2 tablespoons (30 ml) fish sauce *(nuoc mam)*
1/8 teaspoon (1 ml) ground black pepper
4 tablespoons (60 ml) peanut or vegetable oil
3 shallots, sliced
2 carrots, cut into thin strips
1/2 cup (125 ml) water
1 large onion, thinly sliced lengthwise
1 celery stalk, cut on the diagonal into 1-inch
   (3 cm) pieces
1 cup (250 ml) snow peas
Fish sauce *(nuoc mam)* and ground black pepper
   to taste

Trim cartilege from kidneys. Cut kidneys into 1/2-inch (1.5 cm) pieces and combine with 1 table-spoon (15 ml) of the fish sauce and the black pepper and let stand 30 minutes. Heat the oil in a wok or skillet and stir-fry the shallots until browned. Add the kidneys and stir-fry until cooked, about 2 minutes. Remove from the pan with a slotted utensil and set aside. Add the remaining 2 tablespoons (30 ml) oil to the pan and stir-fry the carrots for 2 minutes. Add the water and onions and stir-fry until the onions are almost cooked. Add the celery, snow peas and remaining 1 tablespoon (15 ml) fish sauce and stir-fry 1 minute. Return kidneys to pan and season to taste with fish sauce. Transfer to a serving dish and sprinkle with black pepper.

TRUNG CHIEN
Pork and Eggs

8 ounces (250 g) ground pork
2 tablespoons (30 ml) fish sauce *(nuoc mam)*
1 small onion, finely chopped
1/8 teaspoon (1 ml) ground black pepper
5 eggs, beaten
2 tablespoons (30 ml) peanut oil, or as needed

Combine the ground pork, fish sauce, onion and black pepper and mix well. Add the eggs and mix again. Heat the oil in a skillet and pour about one fourth of the egg mixture (or one eighth if you wish smaller "pancakes") into the hot oil and spread it evenly in the pan. Press the edges of the "pancake" with a spatula so the egg does not run over the pan and cook only as many at a time as you can without crowding them. When the underside is browned, turn and brown the second side. Remove from the skillet and repeat until all of the pork mixture is used.

THIT KHO NUOC DUA
Pork with Coconut Milk

1 pound (500 g) pork shoulder with some fat and
    skin, cut into 1-1/2-inch (4 cm) cubes
3 tablespoons (45 ml) fish sauce *(nuoc mam)*
1/8 teaspoon (1 ml) ground black pepper
3 shallots, thinly sliced
2 cups (500 ml) coconut milk
Fish sauce *(nuoc mam)* to taste
Bean sprout pickle (following)

Combine the meat, fish sauce, black pepper and shallots and let stand 30 minutes. Put the coconut milk in a saucepan and simmer about 5 minutes, or until it becomes light brown. Add the meat to the coconut milk and continue to simmer, uncovered, until meat is very tender and reddish brown in color, about 1-1/2 hours. Add a little water if too much of the liquid cooks away. Season to taste with fish sauce. Serve with bean sprout pickle.

Bean sprout pickle Dissolve 2 teaspoons (10 ml) salt in 1/2 cup (125 ml) water and pour over 8 ounces (250 g) bean sprouts. Let stand 24 hours; drain before serving.

NEM NOUNG
Barbecued Pork

Pork balls

3 ounces (90 g) pork fat
1 pound (500 g) finely ground pork
1-1/2 teaspoons (7 ml) salt
2 teaspoons (10 ml) sugar
6 garlic cloves, finely chopped
1 tablespoon (15 ml) tapioca flour
1/8 teaspoon (1 ml) ground black pepper

Sauce

2 tablespoons (30 ml) fermented black beans
   (tuong), mashed
1 tablespoon (15 ml) peanut oil
3/4 cup (175 ml) water
1 tablespoon (15 ml) sugar, or more to taste
Chopped fresh red chili pepper (optional)
1 cup (250 ml) unsalted roasted peanuts, crushed

Lettuce leaves
Cucumber, peeled and cut into thin strips
Variety of fresh mint leaves
Rice paper rounds, cut into fourths

To make the pork balls, boil the pork fat in water to cover until cooked. Cut the fat into strips about 1 inch (3 cm) long and as thick as a wooden pick. Combine the ground pork, salt, sugar, garlic, tapioca flour, black pepper and pork fat strips and mix well. Form the meat mixture into balls, using about 1 tablespoon (15 ml) to form each. Place on a baking sheet and bake in a preheated 300°F (150°C) oven 10 minutes. Remove from the oven and thread onto bamboo skewers that have been presoaked in water; set aside.

While the pork balls are baking, make the sauce. Combine the black beans, oil, water, sugar and chili pepper in a small pan and boil a few minutes, stirring to dissolve sugar. Taste and adjust seasoning to taste with sugar; set aside.

Grill the skewered pork balls over a low charcoal fire until golden brown. While they are cooking, arrange the lettuce leaves, cucumber strips and mint on a platter. Place the rice paper triangles on a plate and sprinkle them with water so they are pliable. Arrange the skewers on a platter and place near the vegetables. Stir the crushed peanuts into the sauce and transfer to a bowl. Each diner takes a piece of rice paper, tops it with a lettuce leaf, some cucumber and mint and a meatball, rolls it up and dips into the sauce before eating.

GAN HEO NUONG
Charcoal-broiled Pork Liver

8 ounces (250 g) pork liver, cut into slices 1-1/2 by
1 by 1/16 inch (4 cm by 3 cm by 1.5 mm)
8 ounces (250 g) pork shoulder well marbled with
fat, cut into slices 1-1/2 by 1 by 1/16 inch (4
cm by 3 cm by 1.5 mm)
3 tablespoons (45 ml) fish sauce *(nuoc mam)*
1/8 teaspoon (1 ml) garlic powder
1/8 teaspoon (1 ml) ground black pepper
3 shallots, crushed

Combine the pork liver, pork shoulder, fish sauce,
garlic powder, black pepper and shallots and let
stand 1 hour. Alternately skewer the liver and meat
slices onto bamboo skewers that have been presoaked in water. Grill over a charcoal fire until
browned. Serve as an hors d'oeuvre.

Variation Substitute beef liver for the pork liver.

GAN BO XAO HANH
Pork Liver and Onions

1 pound (500 g) pork liver, cut into slices 1-1/2 by
1 by 1/8 inch (4 cm by 3 cm by 3 mm)
2 tablespoons (30 ml) fish sauce *(nuoc mam)*
1/8 teaspoon (1 ml) ground black pepper
3 tablespoons (45 ml) peanut or vegetable oil
1 cup (250 ml) water
4 medium onions, sliced lengthwise 1/16 inch (1.5
mm) thick
Fish sauce *(nuoc mam)* and ground black pepper
to taste

Combine the liver, 1 tablespoon (15 ml) of the fish
sauce and the black pepper and let stand 30 minutes. Heat the oil in a wok or skillet, add the liver
and water and stir-fry until liver is almost cooked.
Add the onions and the remaining 1 tablespoon
(15 ml) fish sauce and stir-fry 2 minutes, or until
liver is cooked. The onions should not be too soft.
Season with fish sauce to taste. Transfer to a serving dish and sprinkle with black pepper.

Variation Substitute beef liver for the pork liver.

OC HEO HAP
Steamed Pork Brain

8 ounces (250 g) pork brain
2 tablespoons (30 ml) fish sauce *(nuoc mam)*
1 egg, beaten
1/8 teaspoon (1 ml) ground black pepper
3 shallots, chopped, or
2 teaspoons (10 ml) chopped onion
1/2 teaspoon (2 ml) monosodium glutamate
(optional)

Rinse the pork brain under cold running water and
remove arteries and outer membranes with the
point of a sharp knife. (Some cooks prefer to leave
the membrane on, so you may eliminate this step.)
The brain should be free of any trace of blood.
Place the brain in a shallow bowl and break it up
with a fork. Mix in the fish sauce, egg, black
pepper, shallots or onion and monosodium glutamate. Steam over gently boiling water 15 to 20
minutes, or until brain is firm and has whitened.

CA CHUA NHOI THIT
Tomatoes Stuffed with Pork

8 ounces (250 g) ground pork
2 tablespoons (30 ml) fish sauce *(nuoc mam)*
1 onion, finely chopped
1/8 teaspoon (1 ml) ground black pepper
8 tomatoes
Peanut or vegetable oil

Combine the pork, fish sauce, onion and black pepper and set aside. Cut the stem ends off the tomatoes and remove the pulp. (Save the pulp for use in another recipe.) Turn the tomatoes upside down to drain well, then stuff with the pork mixture. Heat a few tablespoons (30 to 45 ml) of oil in a skillet and fry the tomatoes meat side down until meat is nicely browned. Turn tomatoes meat side up and cook until tomatoes are just soft.

Note The stuffed tomatoes may also be baked or steamed. To bake, arrange in a deep baking dish and cook in a 325°F (160°C) oven for 30 minutes. To steam, arrange in a deep bowl and steam over gently boiling water 25 to 30 minutes.

OC HEO CHIEN
Fried Pork Brain

8 ounces (250 g) pork brain
4 eggs, beaten
1 tablespoon (15 ml) flour
2 teaspoons (10 ml) chopped onion
2 tablespoons (30 ml) fish sauce *(nuoc mam)*
1/8 teaspoon (1 ml) ground black pepper
2 tablespoons (30 ml) peanut oil, or as needed

Rinse the pork brain under cold running water and remove arteries and outer membranes with the point of a sharp knife. (Some cooks prefer to leave the membrane on, so you may eliminate this step.) The brain should be free of any trace of blood. Place the brain in a bowl and break it up with a fork. Mix in the eggs, flour, onion, fish sauce and black pepper. Heat the oil in a skillet and pour in about one fourth of the brain mixture, spreading it evenly in the pan. Press the edges of the "pancake" with a spatula so the egg does not run over the pan and cook only as many as you can at a time without crowding them. (You can also make smaller "pancakes" if you wish.) Cook until browned on the underside, then turn to brown the second side. Remove from the skillet and repeat until all of the brain mixture is cooked.

Sweets

CHE BAP
Corn Sweet Soup

3 ears of corn
1 quart (1 L) water
5 tablespoons (75 ml) sugar, or more to taste

Using a sharp knife, slice the corn kernels from the cobs. Put the corn kernels in a blender container and blend until smooth. Add the water to blended mixture and mix thoroughly. Line a sieve with cheesecloth or paper toweling and strain the corn mixture through it. Put the strained mixture in a saucepan and add the sugar. Cook over medium heat, stirring constantly, 20 minutes. More sugar may be added to taste. Serve hot or cold.

Variation To make a thicker soup, dissolve 1 tablespoon (15 ml) tapioca flour in 3 tablespoons (45 ml) water. Stir into soup the last few minutes of cooking.

CHE KHOAI LANG
Sweet Potato Sweet Soup

2 medium sweet potatoes, peeled and cut into 1/2-inch (1.5 cm) pieces (about 2 cups or 500 ml)
5 cups (1.25 L) water
Sugar and vanilla extract to taste

Combine the sweet potatoes and water in a saucepan and simmer, uncovered, until tender, about 30 minutes. Add sugar and vanilla extract to taste and simmer 5 minutes longer. Serve hot or cold.

Mung Bean Sweet Soup Substitute 1/2 cup (125 ml) mung dahl (dried mung bean halves without skin) for the sweet potatoes. Proceed as directed in the recipe, simmering the beans until they are very tender, about 40 minutes.

BASICS
of Southeast Asian Cooking

STIR-FRYING

Though commonly thought of with reference to Chinese food preparation, stir-frying is a popular cooking technique in many Asian cultures. Basically, it is rapid cooking in very little oil over high heat. It conserves both fuel and natural vitamins because of the short cooking time, and if properly done, will result in tender but crisp vegetables and moist, flavorful meats and seafood.

Before you begin, have all of your ingredients at hand: the meat, seafood and/or vegetables cut, the sauces mixed, the seasonings measured. Once you have begun, there will be no time to search for a missing seasoning or slice a vegetable. Heat a wok or large heavy skillet over high heat until very hot. Add the oil and heat until it is almost smoking. Now add the ingredients in the order specified in the recipe. Generally, first you will add the ingredients designed to flavor the oil, such as chili peppers, garlic and ginger, then the meat and/or vegetables. As the ingredients cook, you must move them rapidly over the surface of the wok with chopsticks or a long-handled metal spatula so that they receive even heat.

Some recipes specify that once the last of the ingredients have been added, the wok is covered and the dish is allowed to cook *briefly* until done. When covered, the heat can be turned down to medium high if there is any danger of the dish scorching.

STEAMING

There are many pans available specifically designed for steaming. They are generally composed of two pans that stack, much like a double boiler, but with perforations in the bottom of the top pan. If you are steaming plain vegetables, the vegetables can be placed directly on the perforated pan bottom. If you are steaming a prepared dish, the vessel holding the food is set on the bottom of the top pan. Water is added to the bottom pan, the pan is covered, the water is brought to a boil, and as it boils, the steam that escapes through the perforations of the top pan cooks the food.

Bamboo steamers, popular in Asia, are circular baskets with tightly fitting lids, slatted bottoms and rimmed bases that hold the bottoms of the baskets above the steaming water. A prepared dish is set in the bamboo basket, the basket is covered and then set in a wok or other vessel to which the steaming water has been added. The rimmed bases also permit the baskets to be stacked, so that a number of dishes can be steamed at the same time.

A steamer unit can also be easily improvised. Inexpensive collapsible metal steaming baskets with legs can be placed in any sized pot. You can also create a simple stand, such as a tuna fish can with both ends removed, on which to set the dish containing the food to be steamed. An additional alternative is to stand a colander in a large pot. No matter which method you use, the pot must have a tightly fitting lid so that no steam will escape.

The steaming water should be only about one inch (3 cm) deep if you are using a double pan steamer, or within one inch (3 cm) of the bottom of the vessel holding the food to be steamed if you are using an improvised setup. Bring the water to a boil before you start timing the cooking. If the dish you are preparing has a particularly long cooking time, check from time to time to be sure that the water level remains constant.

HOW TO COOK RICE

Rice is the most important food in the daily diet of Southeast Asians. In Thailand, Indonesia and Vietnam, long-grain white rice is preferred, and when properly cooked, the kernels should be dry and separate. The absorption method described here is the most commonly used cooking method in these countries, though the Indonesians also often steam their rice. Electric rice cookers will make perfect rice every time, and if you have one, you may prefer to use it rather than cook the rice on the stove. Simply follow the directions supplied with the appliance.

There is considerable controversy about whether or not to wash rice. Some feel that rice should be washed with several changes of cold water until the water is clear in order to rid it of any dirt and for it to cook properly. Others feel that this washes away many of the nutrients and is thus wasteful. You can decide for yourself.

For a yield of six cups (1.5 L) of cooked rice, wash two cups (500 ml) of rice, if you're washing it, and put into a heavy, medium-sized saucepan. Add four cups (1 L) of water to the pan and bring to a boil over high heat. When the water has evaporated from the surface, turn the heat very low, cover and cook about 15 minutes if a gas stove is used. If an electric stove is used, turn down the heat before all of the water has evaporated from the surface, since it takes longer for the heating unit to react to temperature adjustments. With an electric stove, the cooking time may also be slightly longer. When all of the water is absorbed, the kernels should be tender and fluffy. Fluff lightly with chopsticks or a fork before serving.

The ratio of rice to water is also a source of controversy. The amounts prescribed in the preceding paragraph will work, but other cooks find that an equal amount of rice and water works best. Wash the rice, combine in a saucepan with the water and bring to a boil. Immediately turn the heat to low and cover the pot. If all the water evaporates and the rice is not yet tender, add a quarter cup (60 ml) boiling water, re-cover and cook until tender. Of course, you can also use the ratio of water to rice that works best for you. Plus, rice varies from crop to crop and each cooks a little bit differently.

If you are cooking more than two cups (500 ml) of rice, add water to cover the rice by about 1-1/2 inches (4 cm).

HOW TO MAKE COCONUT MILK

Many have the mistaken notion that coconut milk is the liquid that is inside the nut itself. This liquid is only occasionally used for cooking (see page 47), however. It is primarily drunk as a refreshing, delicious beverage. Coconut milk is made from the grated meat of the nut.

When you select a coconut, make sure the three dark "eyes" on the round side of the nut are closed, and that when you shake the nut, you hear the gurgle of the liquid inside. Poke a hole through one of the eyes with an ice pick or similar instrument and drain off the liquid. Set the nut on several thicknesses of newspaper, and with a hammer or other heavy implement, give it a few good whacks until the hard shell cracks in half and you can remove the shell. (Some cooks prefer to put the coconut halves in a low oven for about 10 minutes. The heat makes it easier to lift the meat from the shell.) The meat will still be covered by a thin brown skin. With a sharp paring knife, peel the skin from the meat. Cut the meat into chunks and grate it by hand, in a blender or in a food processor fitted with a metal blade.

To make the coconut milk, cover the grated coconut meat with an equal amount of boiling water and let it steep until cool enough to handle, then knead with your hands until the liquid is milky white. Strain through a very fine strainer or cheesecloth into a clear glass container. If the recipe calls for coconut cream, let the milk stand for a while and a rich layer will rise to the top. This is the "cream" and can be easily scooped off. The remaining liquid is the coconut milk and can be used whenever coconut milk is called for in this book. (If you do not specifically need the cream, do not allow the liquid to separate and use it all as coconut milk.) You can also differentiate between thick coconut milk, that is, milk from the first extract, and thin coconut milk, milk that is made by repeating the extraction procedure using the same grated coconut that was used for extracting the thick milk. For those wanting a particularly rich coconut milk, use cow's milk or thin cream in place of the boiling water.

If you are lucky enough to have a coconut grater such as those used in Asia, preparing the coconut is even simpler. The easiest type to use requires you only to crack the nut in half. The grater clamps onto a table or counter much like a juicer. With one hand, you hold the coconut half onto the blade head while you turn a handle with the other hand. The sharp serrated blades grate the coconut meat easily right down to the brown skin.

If fresh coconuts are not available, you can use *unsweetened* dessicated (dried) grated coconut in the same manner as the fresh, though the resulting taste is not as good. You can also purchase canned coconut milk on the shelf or in the freezer container of a market specializing in the foods of Southeast Asia or in some supermarkets.

HANDLING CHILI PEPPERS

Fresh hot chili peppers must be handled with care, as their volatile oils will make your skin and eyes burn. Some cooks even wear rubber gloves to preclude any chance of damaging their skin, and if you have particularly sensitive skin, their use is recommended.

To begin, rinse the peppers under cold running water. Make a shallow cut to remove the stem end. If you wish to remove the seeds (they are the hottest part of the pepper), pull them out through the opening. If the pepper is to be shredded, split it lengthwise and cut it into matchstick-length strips. Alternately, mince, chop or cut into rings as specified in the recipes.

Once you have finished cutting the chilies, immediately wash your hands with soap and warm water. If your skin continues to "tingle" or a burning sensation persists, wash your hands again. Be careful not to touch your face or eyes at any point while working with the peppers.

Dried chili peppers are much safer to handle than fresh. If you wish to seed them, simply cut off the stem end and shake out the seeds, then proceed as directed in the recipe. If you are directed to soak them before cutting or grinding them, immediately wash your hands with soap and warm water when you have finished handling them. Although dried chili peppers do not have the volatile oils that make working with fresh ones so precarious, they have plenty of "heat" and flavor when cooked.

Many of the recipes in this book direct the cook to heat the chili peppers, usually in oil or coconut milk, until "pungent." When doing this, be careful not to inhale the rising fumes as they can cause a searing sensation in your nose and throat.

HOW TO FOLD AN EGG ROLL

The following is a simple four-step procedure for folding egg rolls. Though these steps are shown using the large rice paper round, this same basic procedure can be applied if using a quarter-circle wrapper or a square wrapper (see instructions in recipes).

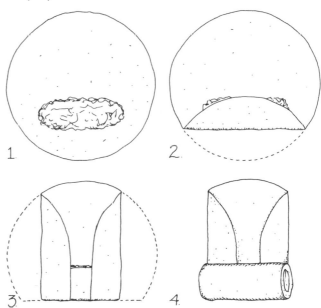

EQUIPMENT

You need no special kitchen equipment to prepare the recipes in this book. There are, however, a few items that will make the job easier.

The most important of these is the wok. Made of iron, its spherical shape permits the even high heat cooking necessary for successful stir-frying, and its high sides allow you to stir the food without fear of it spilling over the sides. Its use is not confined to stir-frying, however. It is equally adaptable for steaming or for the simmering of curries or stews.

There are two basic wok styles—with a single long wooden handle and with two small metal handles—and the choice is solely personal preference. There are also flat-bottomed woks for use on electric stoves and electric "appliance" woks with Teflon coatings. The latter are to be avoided as they do not reach sufficient temperature for sealing in meat juices and the degree of heat cannot be adjusted as quickly as is sometimes necessary when stir-frying.

You must "season" a new wok before you use it. This is a rather simple procedure: Wash it well with hot water and detergent, rinse well and dry over high heat. Rub the inside surface thoroughly with peanut or vegetable oil and place over high heat about one minute. Rinse with plain hot water and place over high heat again. Repeat the procedure, beginning with rubbing the inside surface with oil, several times. The oil will fill the "pores" of the metal, creating a finish to which foods will not stick.

Once this seasoning process is completed, never wash the wok with soap or detergents as this will ruin the seasoning. The inside surface of the wok will gradually darken as you use it more and more. Do not be tempted to scrub it clean: The blacker it is, the better it is to cook in. Of course, any heavy iron skillet can be seasoned and used in place of a wok, but the practical design of this cooking vessel makes it a useful addition to any kitchen.

A Chinese-style cleaver and a heavy wooden cutting board will also be useful additions to your kitchen. If you are not accustomed to using a cleaver, you may initially be put off by its massiveness, but with practice you will find it to be the most efficient tool for slicing, chopping, shredding and dicing ingredients. A French chef's knife will work if you feel more comfortable using one.

The mortar and pestle are traditional tools in the Southeast Asian kitchen. They are principally used for grinding spices, such as for Thai curry mixtures, or for grinding meats and fish to a paste. A blender can replace the mortar and pestle in most instances, though it is sometimes necessary to add a little liquid to dry ingredients if the motor begins to labor.

Long-handled frying "spoons" or "shovels" are good for moving the food about in the wok. A slotted spoon or spatula is handy for removing foods from deep oil or other liquid. Long wooden chopsticks are multipurpose: They are good for stirring foods as they cook, for grasping and turning foods in deep liquids and for beating eggs or mixing other ingredients in a bowl. Standard saucepans are good for cooking soups and you will need a vessel suitable for steaming (see page 150). Aside from these few items, which are only suggestions, any modestly equipped kitchen will suffice for the preparation of the recipes in this book.

Mail-Order Sources

The following firms handle mail-order requests for canned and bottled ingredients and dried herbs and spices. You are advised to write to the firm nearest you and request information on the products available and shipping arrangements. Some firms have a minimum amount, such as $10, that must be ordered for fulfillment.

VIETNAMESE

Oriental Store of Raleigh
3121 North Boulevard
Kings Plaza Shopping Center
Raleigh, NC 27604

Mekong Center
3107 Wilson Boulevard
Arlington, VA 22201

Tien Nha Trang
3709 H-G-F West Bank
  Expressway
New Orleans, LA 70058

Mekong
17 South Fourth Street
San Jose, CA 94103

Saigon Market
42 South Sixth Street
San Jose, CA 94103

Wa Sang
663 South King Street
Seattle, WA 98104

King Chong Lung
617 South King Street
Seattle, WA 98104

Uwajimaya
15555 N.E. 24th
Bellevue, WA 98007

THAI

Bangkok Market
4804 Melrose Avenue
Los Angeles, CA 90029

Siam Grocery
2745 Broadway
New York City, NY 10025

INDONESIAN

Catli's Oriental Market
400 Moffett Boulevard
Mountain View, CA 94040

Haig's
642 Clement Street
San Francisco, CA 94118

The Hollinda Co.
9544 Las Tunas Drive
Temple City, CA 91780

Holland Dutch
6911 West Roosevelt Road
Berwyn, IL 60402

Glossary

The items listed here can all be found in markets featuring the foods of Thailand, Vietnam and Indonesia, many Chinese markets and through the mail-order sources on page 155. Many of them can also be found in well-stocked supermarkets. There will usually be more than one brand to choose from, and often times the choice will be one of personal taste rather than quality. As you become familiar with some of the more exotic foods, your selection of them will become easier. Only those items not fully explained when used in a recipe are included here.

Agar-agar   See page 104.

Aromatic ginger   See Ginger, aromatic.

Asem   See Tamarind.

Asian chili powder   See Chili powder, Asian.

Bamboo shoot   The shoots of young bamboo plants harvested before they break through the soil, the young tender winter ones the most prized. Available water packed in cans and bottles whole or sliced; the Thai and Japanese brands are generally the best. After opening, store refrigerated in water to cover up to 1 week, changing water daily. The shoots are also available dried in long strips. These strips must be cut into smaller pieces before cooking; cooking time is much longer than for the canned variety.

Bamee   See Noodles, wheat.

Basil   Thai, *by holapa;* Indonesian, *kemangi.* Asian variety of sweet basil, the fragrant, green-leaved herb popular in Mediterranean cooking. Easily grown from seed outdoors or as a windowsill plant indoors.

Bean curd, fresh   Made from puréed soybeans. Available in cream-colored cakes approximately 3 inches (8 cm) square and 1/2 to 3/4 inch (1.5 to 2 cm) thick. There are two principal types: the Chinese *(dow foo)* and the Japanese *(tofu).* The former is firmer than the latter and better for stir-frying. The Japanese variety is more delicate and sweeter and is suitable for dishes with substantial broth. For recipes in this book, the firm Chinese bean curd cake is preferred. Rinse well after purchase and cover with cold water; store in the refrigerator, changing the water daily. Will keep up to 1 week.

Bean curd, canned cured   Much stronger in flavor than fresh bean curd; similar to a pungent cheese. Available in cans and bottles; often prepared with chili peppers.

Bean sauce, Chinese   See Soybean condiment.

Bean sprout   Most commonly sprouted mung beans, though sprouted soybeans are also sometimes available and can be used. Avoid using the canned variety.

Bean-thread noodles   Thai, *wun;* Vietnamese, *mien.* Also called cellophane noodles, pea starch noodles. Dry, thin, translucent noodles made from green mung beans. Usually soaked in hot water, then cooked briefly until tender. May also be deep-fried *without* presoaking. Sold by weight in looped skeins (2 to 8 ounces or 60 to 250 g).

Black beans, fermented   Vietnamese, *tuong,* Chinese; *dow see.* Also called salted black beans, black bean sauce. Heavily salted soybeans available in cans, jars and plastic bags. Rinse to remove excess salt before using. Store refrigerated.

Bok choy   See Chinese cabbage.

By holapa   See Basil.

By kaprow   See Mint.

By maglood   See Citrus leaf, dried.

Bun   See Rice vermicelli.

Cabbage, Chinese   Chinese, *bok choy.* Also called Chinese chard. Leafy, dark green vegetable with white stalks. The younger the head, the more tender the leaves and stalks.

Cabbage, Napa   Also called Chinese lettuce, celery cabbage. Tightly packed head, yellow to light green in color; approximately 10 to 12 inches (25 to 30 cm) tall.

Cayenne pepper   See Chili pepper.

Chili pepper   Used principally for flavoring, either whole or cut up. In general, one may use any of the peppers usually available fresh in the market for the recipes in this book—Anaheim, Fresno, yellow wax, *jalapeño, serrano,* etc. The long red cayenne pepper or the purplish-black ones popular in the Mediterranean area are good for Thai curry pastes and *jalapeños* and *serranos* are good for very spicy dishes. The small dried red chili peppers are very hot. They may be added to dishes whole, chopped or powdered; the latter form is also used as a table condiment. The most popular dried chilies include the *serrano,* the Japanese *santaka,* the small cayenne and the Thai *prikeenoh* (the hottest of the lot, sometimes called bird's eye chilies). For instructions on handling, see page 153.

Chili powder, Asian Unlike Mexican chili powder, which is a combination of spices, Asian chili powder is pure ground chili peppers. If unable to obtain, ground cayenne pepper may be substituted, or you may make your own with dried *prikeenoh* chilies. Put them in a flat pan placed over medium heat until dark and pungent, then pulverize in a mortar or blender.

Chili sauce, Thai sweet See Sweet chili sauce, Thai.

Chinese cabbage See Cabbage, Chinese.

Chinese leek See Leek, Chinese.

Citrus leaf, dried Thai, *by maglood;* Indonesian, *djeroek poeroet.* The dried leaves of the Far Eastern wild lime tree. For the Thai recipes, substitute freshly grated lime or lemon rind in an amount equal to twice the volume of the leaves, though the flavor will not be as good.

Citrus peel, dried Thai, *pew maglood.* Dried peel of the Far Eastern wild lime tree. For the Thai recipes, substitute freshly grated lime or lemon rind in an amount equal to twice the volume of the peel, though the flavor will not be as good.

Coconut cream The creamy layer that settles to the top of freshly made coconut milk. See page 152.

Coconut liquid The liquid inside the nut. A delicious beverage and occasionally used in cooking.

Coconut milk Creamy liquid made from freshly grated coconut meat. For directions on how to make, see page 152. Also available in cans.

Coriander Used both fresh and dried; a member of the parsley family. The leafy green herb, which resembles flat-leaved parsley, is quite pungent. Called Chinese parsley and *cilantro,* it is often used as a garnish as well as a flavoring. The ground seeds are an important part of Thai curry blends and Indonesian spice mixtures. Easily grown from seed.

Cumin Available whole and ground; indispensible in curry mixtures.

Da kry See Lemon grass.

Djeroek poeroet See Citrus leaf, dried.

Dow jeeoh dam See Soybean condiment.

Dried bamboo shoot See Bamboo shoot.

Dried shrimp paste See Shrimp paste, dried.

Fish sauce Thai, *nam bla;* Vietnamese, *nuoc mam.* A thin, salty, brown sauce made by salting down small fish that are packed in wooden barrels. The liquid or extract that "runs off" is collected and bottled as fish sauce. A mainstay of Thai and Vietnamese food, the Vietnamese type is darker and generally more pungent than the Thai. Though the odor is strong when uncooked, the flavor mellows when cooked.

Five-spice powder   Fragrant, reddish brown spice mixture that combines star anise, fennel, cinnamon, cloves and Szechwan peppercorns.

Galangal   Thai, *ka;* Indonesian, *laos.* A brown root with white flesh similar in appearance to ginger but more medicinal in flavor. Available dried in slices and powdered.

Gapee   See Shrimp paste, dried.

Ginger root   The gnarled root of the ginger plant with light brown skin and white flesh. Pungent and hot if used in excess. When recipe calls for a "slice," cut a very thin piece about 1 inch (3 cm) in diameter. Peel before chopping or shredding. The root is also dried and ground, though substituting the ground for the fresh is not advised unless the recipe so states.

Ginger, aromatic   Thai, *kachai;* Indonesian, *kentjoer.* Also known as lesser galangal. Available dried in slices and powdered. Stronger in flavor than galangal, which see.

Ginger, pickled   Thinly sliced ginger root preserved in a vinegar brine. Available in bottles in Chinese and Japanese markets.

Glutinous rice   Also called sweet rice, sticky rice. A short-grain white rice that becomes sticky when cooked. Requires soaking and longer cooking than regular rice.

Jalapeño   See Chili pepper.

Ka   See Galangal.

Kachai   See Ginger, aromatic.

Kemiri nut   Also called candlenut. A hard, oily nut popular for use in Indonesian dishes. In appearance resembles the Hawaiian macadamia nut.

Kentjoer   See Ginger, aromatic.

Ketjap   See Soy sauce, Indonesian style.

Kroepoek   See page 24.

Leek, Chinese   Much smaller than the Western leek. More tender and delicate in flavor. Deep green with flat leaves; resembles green onions in appearance. Flavor hints of garlic as well as onion.

Lemon grass Thai, *da kry;* Indonesian, *sereh;* Vietnamese, *xa.* Also known as citronella. Tall grass with sharp-edged leaves; grows in clumps. Stalks are available ground and in pieces. The stalks may be pulverized in a mortar or blender container. Easily grown from seed.

Lotus seed Vietnamese, *hat sen.* Seeds of the lotus plant. Resemble large round peanuts, with dark green skin when fresh and dark brown when dried. Can be eaten raw when very young. Remove skins before adding to any dish by boiling the seeds in water to loosen the skins. The seed itself is white and of delicate flavor.

Me See Tamarind.

Mien see See Soybean condiment.

Mint Thai, *by kaprow.* An Asian variety of bergamont mint. Available fresh and dried; easily grown from seed.

Monosodium glutamate Also called Aji-no-moto, Accent, Vetsin, which are brand names. White crystals similar in appearance to coarse salt. Used ubiquitously throughout Asia in urban areas (less so in rural areas), but maligned in the United States as an odious chemical additive. Originally extracted from dried seaweed, of which monosodium glutamate is a major component, it is now made synthetically. The "Chinese food syndrome," a strange vasomotor head-and-neck ache, will affect some who eat too much of this substance. Using the freshest and tastiest ingredients available will obviate the need for this seasoning; therefore, it has been noted as optional in all recipes that call for it.

Mushroom, dried Also called Chinese black mushroom. The flavor of these mushrooms is quite distinct; the European dried mushrooms cannot be substituted. Sizes range from less than 1 inch (3 cm) to about 2 inches (5 cm); sold by weight. Soak in water until pliable before using.

Mushroom, shiitake Large brown Japanese mushrooms available both fresh and dried. Soak the dried ones in water until pliable before using.

Mushroom, straw Tiny cultivated mushrooms with a sheathlike cap. Available in cans.

Nahm mahn hoi See Oyster sauce.

Nam bla See Fish sauce.

Nam prik Thai generic name for dozens of dipping sauces and condiment mixtures that are served with salads, cooked vegetables and meats. The simplest is *nam bla* (fish sauce) to which chili powder or fresh chopped chilies are added. *Nam prik gapee* incorporates dried shrimp paste. *Nam prik pow* (chili in oil) is a paste made from fish, shrimp, chili peppers, onion and oil and is popularly served with shrimp chips and sometimes added to soups.

Napa cabbage   See Cabbage, Napa.

Noodles, rice   Available fresh and dried, the latter usually imported from Malaysia, Thailand and the Philippines. These are flat noodles, about 1/4 inch (6 mm) wide if dried and 1/2 inch (1.5 cm) wide if fresh. For preparation, see individual recipes or follow directions on the package. See also rice vermicelli.

Noodles, wheat   Thai, *bamee;* Vietnamese, *mi.* In areas with a substantial Asian population, these noodles, made with or without egg, can be found fresh. They are, however, most frequently found frozen or dried. Chinese wheat noodles *(mein),* the easiest to find, can be used for any recipe calling for wheat noodles in this book. For preparation, see individual recipes or follow directions on the package.

Onions, French-fried   An important garnish and seasoning for Indonesian food. See page 13.

Oyster sauce   Thai, *nahm mahn hoi.* Popular Chinese sauce and condiment made from oysters cooked in soy sauce and brine.

Petis   See Shrimp sauce.

Pew maglood   See Citrus peel, dried.

Pickled ginger   See Ginger, pickled.

Plum sauce   A sweet Chinese condiment made from plums, chilies and spices. Excellent with duck.

Radish, preserved   Radishes preserved in salt. Interesting, chewy texture. Available in plastic packages.

Red bean paste, Chinese sweet   Paste made from soybeans and sugar. Popular for filling steamed buns, Chinese moon cakes and other sweets.

Rice flour   Flour milled from rice.

Rice flour, sweet   Flour milled from glutinous rice.

Rice noodles   See Noodles, rice.

Rice paper   Large, brittle, paper-thin rounds made from rice flour and water. Dampen to make pliable.

Rice vermicelli   Vietnamese, *bun.* Also called rice sticks. Dry, thin, translucent noodles made from rice flour. Usually soaked in hot water, then cooked briefly until tender. May also be deep-fried *without* presoaking. Sold by weight in looped skeins (2 to 8 ounces or 60 to 250 g).

Rice vinegar   Red or white delicate-flavored vinegar. Principally used in Thai recipes; Japanese rice vinegar, though not as delicate, may be substituted.

Rice wine   Sweet wine with a high alcohol content. If unavailable, substitute sherry.

Sambal badjak   Indonesian seasoning and condiment made of chilies and onions. See page 12.

Sereh   See Lemon grass.

Sesame oil   Extract made from toasted sesame seeds. Purchase only the Oriental variety; sesame oil available in health food stores cannot be substituted.

Shiitake mushroom   See Mushroom, shiitake.

Shrimp chip or cracker   See Kroepoek.

Shrimp, dried   Shelled, dried, salty shrimp with pungent flavor. Available in a variety of sizes; the small ones can be used for the recipes in this book. Usually, but not always, soaked before using.

Shrimp paste, dried   Thai, *gapee;* Indonesian, *trassi.* Also called *blachan.* Very pungent, dark gray paste made from fermented prawns and used in many Southeast Asian cuisines. Sold in hard cakes or rolls. Store in container with tightly fitting lid.

Shrimp sauce   Indonesian, *petis.* Also called shrimp paste. A dark, thick, liquid made from fermented prawns. Has a strong odor that mellows when cooked.

Siling labuyo   Small chili peppers (about 3/4 inch or 2 cm) preserved in vinegar. Imported from the Philippines.

Som ma kham   See Tamarind.

Soy sauce   Made from fermented soybeans, wheat flour, salt and sugar. There are a number of grades available; the principal ones are thin (or light) and dark. The former is generally reserved for mixing with delicately flavored ingredients you don't want discolored, the latter for mixing with more strongly flavored ingredients. The saltiness of the soy sauce varies with the brand; however, imported soy sauces are superior to domestic brands.

Soy sauce, Indonesian style   Called *ketjap,* this soy sauce is a very sweet, thick, dark version.

Soybean condiment   Thai, *dow jeeoh dam;* Chinese, *mien see.* Thick brown paste of mashed and whole fermented soybeans. The Chinese brands may be used in the recipes in this book. Sold in jars and cans.

Snow pea   Also called sugar pea. Edible flat pea pod. Cook only a short time to retain crunchiness and vibrant color.

Star anise   Licorice-flavored, star-shaped seed available dried. Sold whole by weight.

Straw mushroom   See Mushroom, straw.

Sweet chili sauce, Thai   Hot and sweet and sour chili sauce heavily seasoned with garlic. Good condiment for egg rolls, or can be used as a marinade for barbecued poultry.

Sweet rice   See Glutinous rice.

Szechwan peppercorns   Also called anise pepper, wild pepper. Very pungent seeds with spicy, hot flavor. Sold whole by weight.

Tamarind   Thai, *som ma kham;* Indonesian, *asem.* Vietnamese, *me.* A tropical fruit tree, the seedpods of which have tough gray-brown shells covering 2 or 3 beans of tamarind. Inside the beans are shiny dark seeds covered with dark brown, slightly sticky flesh. The seeds are discarded and the flesh is rubbed to a thin paste in a little water. The sour taste of the tamarind is similar to the effect one gets by adding lemon juice or vinegar to a dish. Though fresh tamarind can sometimes be found, dried or frozen pulp is more widely available. Combine a piece of the pulp with hot water, mash well and squeeze out the extract. Strain and use extract when recipe calls for tamarind liquid.

Taro root   Starchy potatolike tuber used throughout Asia. Yams or sweet potatoes are good substitutes.

Tempeh   A soybean product in which the beans are fermented but left whole. Sold frozen in cakes about 5 inches (12 cm) square and 1 inch (3 cm) thick. To use, thaw partially to ease cutting.

Trassi   See Shrimp paste, dried.

Tuong   See Black beans, fermented.

Turmeric   A root with brown skin and yellow flesh. Most readily available dried and ground. Gives a beautiful golden color to dishes.

Water chestnuts   Though sometimes available fresh, in which case the brownish black skin must be peeled with a sharp knife, these crisp "kernels" are most readily available canned. Once opened, store refrigerated in water to cover up to 1 week, changing water daily.

Wood fungus   Also called, monkey ears, mouse ears, cloud ears, wood ears. Sold by weight, these dry grayish-brown fungi have a pleasing texture once soaked in water, but have almost no flavor. The "ear" designation comes from their distinctive shape.

Index

Biographical Notes

LAN CAO was born in the town of Namvinh in northern Vietnam. In 1975 she came to the United States and obtained her degree in nutrition from the University of Tennessee in Knoxville. Presently she lives in Raleigh, North Carolina, with her husband and their two children.

JEFFREY DAVIS is an American physician who has lived and traveled extensively in Southeast Asia during the past 10 years doing medical work and research—and collecting recipes. He collaborated on the Thai section of this book with Jintana, a friend from Bangkok.

FRONA DE LANNOY and MAUDY A. HORSTING are sisters who were born to Dutch-Javanese parents on the island of Java in Indonesia, where they lived until 1946 when they went to study in Holland. They came to the United States some 20 years ago and presently live in California.

AUDREY GARWOOD is a Canadian-born painter and printmaker who studied at the Ontario College of Art in Toronto, Rijks Academie in Amsterdam and La Grande Chaumière in Paris. Her works have been widely exhibited throughout Canada and the United States, including 13 one-artist exhibitions. The drawings in this book are from her sketchbook during an extended visit to Southeast Asia.